TRUE CRIMES

CRIMES
OF PASSION

igloo

This edition published in 2010
by Igloo Books Ltd
Cottage Farm
Sywell
NN6 0BJ

www.igloo-books.com

A copy of the British Library Cataloguing-in-Publication
Data is available from the British Library.

10 9 8 7 6 5 4 3 2 1

ISBN 978-0-85734-396-3

Printed and Manufactured in China

Contents

Anibal Almodovar

A serial womanizer who was quick to anger, Anibal Almodovar became so furious at his new wife's insistence that he give up his wayward sexual lifestyle that he killed her just weeks after the wedding. Unfortunately for him, he did not stop to consider that it might not just be witnesses that could place him at the scene of the murder. The evidence that convicted him came from somewhere no one would have suspected.

An extremely handsome man and former sailor, 25-year-old Puerto Rican Anibal Almodovar was working as a porter in New York City when he met a waitress in a Manhattan bar and married her. Two years younger than her new husband and strikingly pretty herself, Louise Almodovar assumed that as a married man her husband would give up the one-night stands

BELOW: An aerial view of Central Park, where Anibal Almodovar dumped the body of his wife Louise.

and frequent flings he had been so used to enjoying. But she was wrong. The couple hadn't been married more than a few weeks when it became apparent to her that Almodovar was still pursuing the same lifestyle; he made few efforts to hide the fact from his wife. She protested and a violent argument broke out, after which Almodovar stormed out of the apartment.

Unwilling to give up on her marriage so quickly, Louise later called him at a local bar and asked to meet so they might try and resolve their problems more calmly. He agreed and told her that he would see her in Central Park. Louise's body was found among tall grass in the famous park on November 2, 1942. The ripped sleeve of her jacket suggested that she had struggled furiously, and the chief medical examiner concluded that she had been throttled by a killer who had placed two fingers from each hand on her windpipe.

Unable to identify the corpse and assuming that it was a random killing committed by one of the many dubious characters that could be found in Central park at night, the police department was initially at a loss. But when reports of a missing woman whose husband was a known cheat and violent bully came in, they scented a murderer.

Almodovar was brought in for questioning and his clothes taken away for examination. The seeds found in the turn-ups of his trousers would later prove crucial in convicting him of his wife's murder.

At first, Almodovar made a full confession, telling police he had lost control when Louise nagged him about seeing other women. He said he had strangled her and left the scene. However, when the case came to trial, on February 24, 1943, he retracted the confession. The police, he said, had forced it out of him under duress. Now he maintained that he had nothing to do with Louise's death.

Unfortunately for him, the seeds that had been found in his trousers were from rare plants growing at the murder scene. They had been planted there as a nursery experiment and could not be found anywhere else in New York. What's more, as a professor of biology and botany explained to the court, as the seeds found on Almodovar's trousers only matured within a week of the murder, the evidence placed Almodovar at site on the night Louise was killed. Anibal Almodovar's was the first case in US legal history to rely on botanical evidence to get a conviction. He was found guilty and sentenced to death in the electric chair.

Tracie Andrews

A former boyfriend would later recall, "When Tracie gets angry her eyes go wild," and the parents of her victim have spoken of their fear that she will kill again if ever released. For Tracie, it seems that rage is never far from the surface and if roused to passion she can be deadly, as Lee Harvey found out.

The relationship of barmaid and former model Tracie Andrews and her fiancé Lee Harvey was a stormy one. Both had tempers and—as neighbors would later tell the police—often had violent arguments. The row they had while driving to their home in Alvechurch near Worcester, England, on December 1, 1996, was no different from the rest, except in the way it ended. Tracie's uncontrollable temper finally snapped completely and, in a frenzy of rage, she pulled a knife and stabbed Harvey 15 times.

Two days later, she appeared at a press conference appealing for information about Harvey's killer. She told the cameras and waiting reporters that Harvey had been the victim of a road rage attack by a man with "staring eyes." Her story was that a "tatty" Ford Sierra had followed them flashing its lights, before drawing level when they stopped. The driver then got out and knifed Harvey. The police described the attack as "particularly vicious" and the killing was highly publicized in the national press.

any witnesses to the road rage attack and not a single member of the public had come forward. All the evidence pointed to the killer being closer at hand.

Even after she had been charged and released on bail, Tracie maintained her story, but she could not stop the truth seeping out. At her trial the jury heard that Harvey had been obsessively jealous over her and accused her of seeing other men. The neighbors told their own stories of screaming rows.

Tracie Andrews was found guilty of murder at Birmingham Crown Court on July 29, 1997. Sentenced to life in prison with the recommendation that she serve a minimum of 14 years, she immediately lodged an appeal claiming she was the victim of a miscarriage of justice because of the publicity about her case. It was thrown out in October 1998.

Two years later, Tracie finally admitted she had killed Lee Harvey, and in 2005 a television documentary was made about the case. A prison source said, "Andrews has… admitted to the murder, which has surprised a lot of people. Although she has accepted her guilt, nobody really believes that she feels much remorse. She sees this as her first step on the way to parole. Andrews is manipulative and devious. Officers believe she will say or do anything to get out of jail."

BELOW: The sleepy village of Alvechurch was shocked by the murder of Lee Harvey in 1996.

ABOVE: Tracie Andrews arriving at Birmingham Crown Court on July 29, 1997, to hear the verdict in her murder trial.

Either wracked with guilt or in fear of being found out, Tracie took a drug overdose the next day, but survived. She was arrested in hospital on December 7, while recovering. The police had been unable to find

Arnold Axilrod

A man whose sexual appetites were matched only by his depravity, dentist Arnold Axilrod drugged his patients so that he could rape them while they were unconscious. He also kept a lover, and when she fell pregnant the evil man decided to terminate the fetus, and his mistress with it.

On the morning of April 23, 1955, John J. Cowles, Jnr., of the Cowles publishing empire was backing his Pontiac out of his garage, in Minneapolis, when he noticed what appeared to be a bundle of clothes in the alley. The "bundle" was the body of a young woman. Her face had been scratched and bruised, and her throat had a bluish mark. Police were called and when they searched the woman's coat pockets found a wallet containing a five-dollar bill, a doctor's prescription slip, and a driver's license. The woman was identified as Elizabeth Mary Moonen aged 21.

An autopsy revealed that she had been strangled, and that Elizabeth had been three months pregnant. It also found traces of semen in her vagina, which suggested that she had had intercourse just prior to her death. It seemed likely that her sexual partner would also be her killer. Here the mystery deepened, for police enquiries found that Elizabeth's husband was a serviceman stationed in Korea.

The starting point in the hunt for Elizabeth's lover was Dr. Glen Peterson who had issued the prescription found in Elizabeth's wallet, and he immediately pointed police in the right direction. He told them that she had named the baby's father as local dentist Arnold Axilrod, 49, who had a reputation as something of a ladies' man.

In fact, Axilrod was much more sleazy than a simple womanizer. His surgery was above a seedy nightclub called the Hoop De Do, and his patients were mainly nightclub performers and hat-check girls. Despite the fact that he had a spotless reputation, there were doubts about his activities. In late 1954, a phone call had been received by the police during which an anonymous woman told an officer that Axilrod had sedated her to operate on her teeth and then raped her while she was unconscious. But as she refused to give her name or file a complaint, the allegation was never investigated.

Axilrod buckled quickly under police questioning. He admitted that he'd given Elizabeth a ride on the evening of her death, and said that the two had quarreled after she accused him of being the father of her child. He claimed she had also threatened to expose him. The next thing he knew, Axilrod continued, was that he'd blacked out and when he came to, Elizabeth was no longer in the car. What he said next surprised the police. When they told him that she had been strangled, Axilrod replied, "If she was strangled, I must have done it. I was the only one there." He later withdrew that statement.

When the case hit the newspapers, 20 women came forward to say they had also been drugged by the dentist. One was Elizabeth's sister who said that Axilrod had talked suggestively to her. Axilrod went on trial for murder in Hennepin County District Court in late 1955. Despite public outrage, the evil dentist was not convicted of murder though. At the end of his trial, the jury found Axilrod guilty of manslaughter and given a prison sentence.

Arthur Bagg

When jealousy enters an already unbalanced mind, the results can be tragic. And few minds have been as fevered as Arthur Bagg's. His was a life lived in fantasy, worshipping the mythical Count Dracula, and the murder he committed was every bit as ghastly as any from a horror story.

When 17-year-old Marjorie Patricia Rosebrook's stabbed and mutilated body was found beneath a viaduct outside Johannesburg, South Africa, suspicion immediately settled on her boyfriend, artist Arthur Bagg. The detectives' certainty that they had found the killer hardened when he told them that he hadn't been with Marjorie on the day of the murder—November 23, 1937. In fact, they already had several witnesses who reported that they had seen the couple together.

Determined to get a confession, the police continued to interrogate the 23-year-old. Eventually he broke down and willingly took officers to the scene of the crime, even going so far as to re-enact the killing for them. In a jealous rage over her conduct with another man, he had had stabbed her twice. Nevertheless, that didn't explain the mutilation and there was also the question of Marjorie's missing clothes and the murder weapon. At this point Bagg's co-operation dried up, for the full extent of his lunacy was yet to be uncovered. He tried everything he could to stop a police search of his home, and once there it soon became apparent why.

Beneath the floor of his bedroom was a secret earthen chamber hidden by a trapdoor; a "ritual site" where Bagg worshipped Count Dracula. It was also where he had hidden the murder knife and Marjorie's blood-stained clothing. Along with the incriminating evidence detectives found a piece of leather on which Bagg had carved the words, "I hereby defile the living God and serve only the Dark One, Dracula; to serve him faithfully so I may become one of his faithful servants."

Ironically, it was the evidence that he had tried to conceal that would save Bagg from execution. At his trial, on February 28, 1938, he withdrew his confession to Marjorie Rosebrook's murder and claimed she had committed suicide. He said he had only told police he had killed her to save her from shame. But after two hours deliberation, the jury found Bagg guilty of murder and he was sentenced to death. However, after assessments of his mental state were made—which took into account his strange shrine to the vampire—the sentence was commuted to life imprisonment. Bagg was released in 1947 after serving nine years.

BELOW: Arthur Bagg's obsession with Count Dracula led him to commit the horrendous murder of Marjorie Rosebrook.

Lorena Bobbitt

Although Lorena Bobbitt did not actually kill her husband, she inflicted on him a terrible—and now infamous—wound. In an odd twist of fate, she was not punished for her crime and instead became something of a heroine to feminists.

It was an incident that grabbed headlines around the world. John Wayne and Lorena Bobbitt returned to their home in Manassas, Virginia, on June 23, 1993, after an evening of partying and drinking, and Lorena would later allege that Bobbitt raped her. She told a court that it was just the latest abuse in a long list of others. Her husband was often violent toward her and made no secret of the fact that he was having sex elsewhere. On one occasion, she said that he had forced her to terminate a pregnancy against her wishes. This time, however, John Wayne would pay a terrible price for his behavior.

After the attack, as John lay sleeping, Lorena got out of bed to fetch a glass of water from the kitchen. As the tap was running, she spotted a carving knife and, as she stared at it, the years of abuse that she had suffered at the hands of her husband all came flooding back. Overwhelmed with anger and

ABOVE: Lorena Bobbitt waving to cheering demonstrators as she leaves the Prince William County Courthouse in Manassas, Virginia.

BELOW: The knife used by Lorena Bobbitt to cut off the penis of her husband.

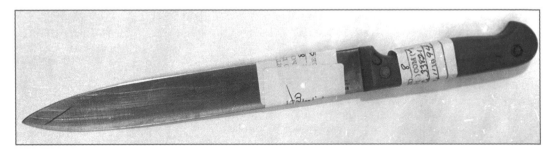

ABOVE: Lorena Bobbitt (left), being escorted from the courtroom in the Prince William County Courthouse, Virginia, following the not guilty verdict.

At this point Lorena came back to her senses, and realizing that she had committed a terrible crime she called the emergency services. Bobbitt was rushed to hospital while police combed the field for his penis. It was eventually found and the police packed it in ice and rushed it to the hospital. It took nine-and-a-half hours in surgery to successfully re-attach the severed body part.

Lorena defended her actions in court by maintaining that she had been the victim of constant abuse. Her lawyers told the jury that suffering from depression and post-traumatic stress disorder she had simply snapped. While John Wayne denied all of his wife's allegations, Lorena was able to supply witnesses to support her claims and she was eventually found not guilty of sexually wounding her husband.

In 1994, it was John's turn to face the judgement of the court. He stood trial for raping Lorena, but he, too, was acquitted.

By 1995 the couple were divorced. Although she had hardly knowing what she was doing, Lorena Bobbitt picked up the knife, walked back to the bedroom, and sliced off more than half of Bobbitt's penis. Then she picked up the severed organ and drove a short distance before throwing it into a field.

tried to avoid media attention, Lorena Bobbitt had by now become a feminist icon, and in the years that followed she founded Lorena's Red Wagon, an organization devoted to bringing an end to domestic violence. She later obtained a degree and gave birth to a daughter by a new partner, though when she and John were both guests on the Oprah Winfrey Show in 2009 she insisted that she would never marry again. John Wayne Bobbitt, however, used his new notoriety

in a different way. He formed a band called The Severed Parts and appeared in adult movies. He also continued to abuse women and after two more court cases for domestic assault was convicted in 2004.

LEFT: John Wayne Bobbitt (center) arriving at the Prince William County Court House for the first day of his wife's trial on charges of malicious wounding.

BELOW: Supporters of Lorena Bobbitt hold signs and shout their support as she leaves the courthouse.

Mary Bolton

From almost the day that she was married, in 1922, Mary Bolton was a dreadful thorn in her husband's side. And as time went on she became more and more unbalanced, to the point where she was willing to kill rather than lose him.

A good-natured, hard working, and patient man Charles Bolton most certainly didn't deserve the woman he married. Almost immediately after the wedding, he realized that he had made a terrible mistake: Mary nagged him constantly and made wild accusations. Each day he went to his office and each night he returned home to face her jealousy. She was convinced that he was having affairs and became so frenzied in her rage that she would even beat him and, on one occasion, slashed his face with a razor. The hapless Bolton was forced to tell police who came to investigate when neighbors reported the violent row that he had cut himself shaving.

None of Mary's accusations was true. Bolton was a decent man and despite his wife's temper tried hard to make their marriage work. His protestations and attempts to calm Mary were futile though, and the strain was affecting his work. His employers even suggested that due to his personal problems he might be better off working for himself.

After enduring her emotional and physical torments for 14 years, Bolton finally came to the end of his tether, and filed for divorce on January 25, 1936. Mary, however, was not going to let him get away so easily and spent months harassing him to change his mind. And when she realized that Bolton was determined to be rid of her, she decided that she would get rid of him first.

Mary bought a revolver on June 11, and drove to her husband's office. All the way her rage grew and by the time she was riding the elevator to the 10th floor her fury was uncontrollable. Finding her husband in his office, Mary fired six shots. As Charles Bolton lay bleeding to death on the floor, she asked, "Why don't you get up and stop faking?"

Mary Bolton was originally sentenced to death in the electric chair but this was later commuted to a sentence of life imprisonment. However, Mary did not fancy spending the rest of her life—perhaps another 40 years—behind bars. She died on August 29, 1943, after slashing her wrists with a pair of scissors.

Lizzie Borden

Not all crimes of passion are triggered by lust or passion turned sour. For Lizzie Borden it was hatred of her stepmother and a domineering father, as well as good old-fashioned greed, which turned her into a brutal killer. Perhaps one of the most famous murderers in history, Borden was never convicted of her crime, but looking back it seems almost impossible that she got away with it. Never able to give a clear account of her whereabouts at the time of the double murder, she was lucky enough to have a judge who owed her defense counsel a favor and she also threw herself on the sympathy of the jury, and their misplaced belief that a mere woman could not have committed such a frenzied slaying.

B orn in Fall River, Massachusetts, in 1860, Lizzie's mother died when she was just two years old. Her father married again, a woman called Abby Gray who was 10 years his junior, and as Lizzie and her sister, Emma, grew up they came to despise their stepmother. To them she was a simple gold-digger who was frittering away their inheritance. Matters came to a head when their father, who was notoriously mean with money gave his wife's sister a large sum to save her from financial ruin. Lizzie wanted revenge.

The opportunity presented itself in the summer of 1892. Emma had gone to stay with friends at the nearby country town of Fairhaven while Lizzie remained at home with just a maid in the house along with Lizzie and her stepmother and father.

On August 4, Lizzie's father was away from the house for a short while. Around 9.30am, Mrs Borden was cleaning the steps to a spare bedroom when she was struck from behind with an axe. The blow to her head was enough to kill her instantly, but eight more rained

ABOVE: A colorized photograph of Lizzie Borden from the late 19th century.

him!" The police were soon on the scene and under questioning, Lizzie's own story changed constantly from the outset. First she said she had been out in the yard when her father was killed, then she "remembered" that she had actually been in the barn. At the inquest that would change again, with Lizzie recalling that she had been in the kitchen when her father returned home. Although at one time she also said she had been on the stairs, she maintained that she had not noticed her stepmother's body there.

Nevertheless, the early investigation focused on John Morse, the brother of Mr Borden's first wife, who had recently stayed with the family for a few days. That avenue of investigation proved short-lived when Morse provided a solid alibi. The police were left with just two suspects—Lizzie and Bridget Sullivan. Quickly they narrowed it down to one as it was established that the maid had no motive for the crime while Lizzie had made no secret of the fact that she hated her stepmother. Her contradictory statements were also arousing suspicion.

By the time Lizzie Borden came to trial in June 1893, public opinion was already behind her. The folk of Massachusetts could not bring themselves to believe that one of their own, a God-fearing woman, could have committed such a crime. Lizzie had also cannily appointed one of the best criminal lawyers in the state to defend her. George Robinson was a former governor of Massachusetts and, crucially, had been responsible for appointing one of the three judges who now sat on the bench before him. The judge repaid the favor by agreeing with Robinson that damning transcripts of Lizzie's questioning at the inquest, during which her story had changed several times, were inadmissible. The prosecution case looked weaker and weaker, having finally to rest on the fact that Lizzie Borden was at the house at the time of the murders and that her evidence was conflicting.

Lizzie and her lawyer did their utmost to secure the jury's sympathy. Midway through the 10-day hearing she appeared to collapse in a faint, while Robinson later pointed to the soberly dressed, neat figure, saying: "To find her guilty, you must believe she is a fiend. Gentlemen, does she look it?" The tactic worked. The jury found Lizzie not guilty and she was set free. On

down in quick succession. The same fate awaited her husband when he returned home an hour or so later; a killing blow was landed and again followed by a ferocious attack on his already dead body. Both heads were later removed for specialist forensic examination, which revealed "injuries consistent with a frenzied, almost psychopathic, attack, although both victims died with the first blow such was the force with which it was delivered."

The alarm was raised when the maid, Bridget Sullivan, heard Lizzie screaming, "Come down, come down. Father's dead. Someone came in and killed

ABOVE: The Borden house in Fall River, Massachusetts where the grisly murders were committed.

Ireland soon after with, it was often said, a large quantity of cash from the late Mr Borden's bank account given to her by Lizzie.

The jury may have been convinced of her innocence, but the public was not so satisfied. and as the years passed it became the widespread belief that Lizzie had gotten away with murder. She may have escaped the law, but for the remainder of her days would be taunted by a popular rhyme: "Lizzie Borden took an axe. And gave her mother forty whacks. When she saw what she had done. She gave her father forty-one!"

Lizzie Borden initially lived with her sister and then by herself until she died aged 67 in 1927. She was buried in the same family plot as those who died on that sweltering August day 35 years before.

being acquitted of murder, she inherited much of her father's money and used it to buy a house in a wealthy suburb. Suspiciously, Bridget Sullivan returned to

Cordelia Botkin

Cordelia was most definitely a "woman scorned." Having won her younger lover, he deserted her and returned to his wife. Love turned to seething fury and when Botkin's attempts to ruin his marriage failed, there was only one course of action left: revenge. Not on the man who had broken her heart, but on the woman who had taken him from her.

At 41 years old, **Cordelia Botkin** was a sophisticated woman of the world. Separated from her wealthy grain broker husband, he nonetheless supported her financially, leaving her free to indulge a busy social life and numerous flirtations. But when she met John Preston Jack Dunning in 1896, she felt a powerful attraction that appeared to be mutual. He was 32, nine years her junior, and a highly regarded reporter for the Associated Press in California. Soon the couple were involved in a passionate affair. It was not Dunning's first, and when his wife found out that once again he was cheating on her, she decided that she had had enough. She left, taking their small daughter away to her father's home. Cordelia was overjoyed. With Mary Dunning out of the picture she could at last take a more public position in her lover's life.

The affair lasted three years. During that time, Dunning began to drink more and more heavily, and became addicted to gambling. Eventually, he was sacked by the Associated Press after embezzling $4,000 dollars to pay gambling debts, and though he found work on local San Francisco newspapers was quickly fired by them too; this time for habitual drunkenness. Homeless and penniless, Dunning was forced to move into the hotel where Cordelia lived. There, he surveyed the wreckage of his life and decided to clean up his act.

Well aware of Dunning's talent, in 1898 the Associated Press agreed to give him another chance and hired him as their lead reporter. It meant leaving San Francisco, but he seemed all too keen to return to the life he'd had before it had all gone so disastrously wrong. Although Cordelia pleaded with him desperately, her agonized pleas fell on deaf ears. Dunning left her, was reconciled with his wife, and left for news assignments in Cuba, where he became a hero at the battle of Santiago Bay when he helped save survivors of the Spanish battleships that were sunk.

BELOW: The California State Prison at San Quentin where Cordelia Botkin lived out her final days.

Already heartbroken, when Cordelia heard of her faithless lover's new success and the mended relationship with his wife, she became incensed with jealousy. Having supported and loved Dunning through all his troubles, it was the final humiliation. At first she tried to vent her rage by sending Mary Dunning anonymous letters that gave intimate details of all her husband's affairs, but it didn't have the effect she had hoped. More radical measures were called for.

One morning, Mary Dunning was delighted to receive a box of candies at her father's home in Delaware. An unsigned note attached said, "With love to yourself and baby," but the fact that the handwriting was the same as the poison-pen letters she had received obviously didn't register. Mary ate three and shared the rest. The candy contained a real poison this time: arsenic. Two days later, Mary was dead, alongside her sister Harriet. Miraculously, four others who had eaten the sweets survived.

It didn't take the police long to follow the trail back to Cordelia. Mary's father noticed that the note accompanying the candy was in the same hand as the poison pen letters his daughter had been receiving, and the box of candy was traced back to San Francisco. Cordelia Botkin denied the murder charges, but the case against her was open and shut. She was convicted in December 1898 and again at a retrial in 1904.

Sentenced to life, she eventually died in 1910 at San Quentin State Prison, her life destroyed by jealousy. And hers was not the only one. If vengeance on the man she loved was what she was after then Cordelia succeeded. The loss of his wife and the ensuing scandal tipped Dunning into a downward spiral. He died, virtually destitute, before she did.

Leone Bouvier

Leone Bouvier's life was one of abuse, and when the man whom she believed would save her from it betrayed her too, it proved too much for her to bear.

The daughter of a drunk father and unsympathetic mother, at 16 years old, Leone Bouvier had already lost her virginity during a fumbled encounter in a field and been taken advantage of by various local lads. Illiterate and unloved, she had little in life to look forward to when she met a 22-year-old garage mechanic named Emile Clenet. For the first time Leone believed that someone cared about her. Clenet would visit her on a Sunday, take a hotel room, and the couple would spend the day making love, taking rests to laugh together and talk about marriage.

But like many a naive young girl, she was deceived. While Clenet certainly enjoyed the promise of certain sex on a Sunday, he had little love for her. Leone had already suspected that he had a cruel streak, but in a haze of love she had made excuses for him. And when she fell pregnant in 1951 she continued to trust him. On hearing the news, Clenet refused to live up to his responsibilities and instead, callously told his teenage lover to get rid of the baby. Leone obediently had a termination. It left her ill; the headaches and depression she had previously suffered from grew so bad that she eventually lost her job at a shoe factory. Her drunk father beat her when he was told that she would no longer be bringing a wage home. In desperation Leone cycled 30 miles to Nantes in the hope of finding comfort in the arms of her lover, but Clenet briskly told her she had broken the "Sundays only" rule and refused to speak to her.

Jobless and abandoned by her lover and family, Leone lived on the streets and earned money for food the only way she could; by prostituting herself. Despite all that had happened she still loved Clenet and hoped against hope that they might marry, but as time passed their meetings became few and far between and, when he did show up, he showed no compassion for her plight. Much of her life was now spent at the docks where she sold her body. Sick, heartbroken, betrayed, and with her thoughts dwelling on revenge, Leone spent what little money she had on a pistol.

Still, disaster might have been averted if Clenet had returned just a little of the love that Leone had given him. But it was not to be. At a final meeting, during which the couple visited a carnival, Clenet announced he was to leave France to work in North Africa. Leone begged him to stay, but he simply shrugged and told her that he would never marry her. In response Leone pulled his reluctant face to hers for a parting kiss. Then she shot him at point-blank range in the neck.

Leone was arrested in a convent at Angers where she had sought shelter with her sister who had become a nun several years before. She was charged with murder and brought to trial in December 1953. Fate still had one final misfortune for her. Although she had killed a man, if anyone deserved to be treated leniently under the French traditions of the *crime passionnel* it was Leone Bouvier. Nevertheless, she was unlucky enough to be assigned an unsympathetic judge. When he heard that her sister was a nun, he chastised Leone for not making anything of her own life, and even the appearance of a drunk father and long-suffering mother in the dock did nothing to sway him. He told her that killing her lover as he bent to kiss her was an act of gross atrocity and took no notice of Leone's weeping or her whispered words, "But I loved him."

After deliberating for just 15 minutes, the jury saved Leone from a death sentence by finding her guilty of murder without premeditation. However, she received the full penalty of the law: a life sentence with a minimum of 20 years to be served.

Elliot Bower

It is rare indeed that someone who confesses to killing a love rival is set free, yet in Paris in the mid-1800s that is exactly what happened. The British defendant used the French plea of crime passionel rather than premeditated murder, and he was set at liberty, with many even agreeing that he had done the honorable thing by slaying his wife's lover.

Like many men of his time, Elliott Bower was a hypocrite whose double standards are easy to see in these more enlightened days. An English foreign correspondent working in Paris, he thought nothing of betraying his wife, Fanny, with a series of women. Such was his arrogance that he hardly bothered keeping his numerous mistresses a secret from her. For the unfortunate Fanny Bower, life became a series of heartbreaks as she discovered time and again that her husband had been cheating on her with yet another. Needless to say, while Bower pleasured himself with the ladies of Paris, his wife was expected to be completely faithful and uncomplaining.

Emotionally crushed after her husband's latest fling was revealed to her, Fanny finally turned in desperation to a close friend of her husband's who had always been kind to her. Saville Morton was also a foreign correspondent, working for a rival newspaper, and during happier times he had become almost part of the family, dining often with the Bowers and accompanying them for Parisian nights out. Now, Morton's relationship with the distressed Fanny deepened into something more and, as time passed, they became lovers. Soon, Fanny fell pregnant.

When the child was born (Fanny's fifth), she instantly declared it to be, "just like Morton!" At first, fearing scandal, Morton stayed away, but his lover's fragile emotional state had been further weakened by the birth of another man's child. She summoned Morton to her bedside and banned her husband from the room. He

must have been suspicious, and his fears were confirmed on the night of October 1, 1852. At last called to his wife's side, he heard her confess in a fevered outburst that he was not the father of her child.

In a frenzy of rage that he—the serial adulterer—should be deceived in his turn, he confronted his former friend. Morton admitted everything. Bower, in a fury, took up a long carving knife and ran him through with it.

To escape punishment Bower deserted his family and fled to England. But soon came the news that French police considered his act a *crime passionnel*, and not premeditated murder. Knowing that this would be treated much more leniently, Bower returned to France and gave himself up. At his trial, which started on December 28, 1852, Bower listened to the heated defense put up by his counsel; that he had been driven to kill because of Morton's seduction of his wife, his close friend's dishonorable and treacherous behavior, and the ultimate humiliation of the birth of a child which was not his. In fact, he was presented to the jury as the real victim of the affair, and the murder of his wife's lover not only understandable, but a deserved punishment and an act of honor.

He was lucky to be tried in a country that prides itself on having the legal defence of a *crime passionnel*. Perhaps he would not have been given such a sympathetic hearing anywhere else. Acquitted of the crime, and virtually hailed as a hero by the French press, Bower left the court a free man.

Martha Bowers

Taking another human life is a terrible crime and one that affects killers in different ways. Some suffer the torture of their own conscience as they realize what they have done, others remain defiant. A few seem to feel no remorse whatsoever. When Martha Bowers husband died she threw herself on his body, weeping hysterically. But less than two hours later she was spotted laughing and joking with her lover.

Martha Bowers married her third—and final—husband in San Francisco in 1902, but such happiness she may have had with Martin Bowers, a bridge builder, did not last long. Martha was not the type to be satisfied with just one man and before her marriage was a year old she was enjoying the attentions of a lover, Patrick Leary. It wasn't long before Bowers became aware of his wife's infidelity, and he insisted that the affair must come to an end.

Soon after, on June 5, 1903, a doctor was called to their home. Martha asked Dr. Carl Von Tiedmann if he could prescribe medicine for her husband saying that he had become ill as a result of ptomaine poisoning caused by eating too much ham. Over the following days, Martin's condition deteriorated until a second doctor was called in. This time, Bowers was taken to a convalescent home and finally he began to recover. After a month he was judged fit to return home. Not long after, he was critically sick again and was rushed to hospital where he died on August 25, with his wife pouring out her grief over his lifeless body.

Harry Bowers—Martin's brother—was perplexed. Something about the death didn't seem quite right. He requested a full postmortem be carried out, which found four grains of undissolved arsenic in Martin Bowers' stomach. By now the possible murder was making news reports and caught the eye of a pharmacist who recalled a woman coming to him on August 20, with a prescription for arsenic. He told police the prescription was memorable because though signed by a Dr. McLaughlin, it was written on a plain sheet of paper and not a normal prescription form. However, the description of the woman the pharmacist gave turned out not to match that of Martha, but it did lead police to her sister, Zylpha Sutton.

In Bowers' home, police found a school composition book with a page torn out. It matched that upon which the phoney prescription had been written and so, too, did the handwriting in the book. The police also heard from witnesses of how Martha had been seen playfully cavorting in public with Patrick Leary less than two hours after the death of her husband.

With further revelations about how Martin Bowers had attempted to put an end to the affair, it was more than enough to condemn her. Martha Bowers was found guilty on January 20, 1904, and sentenced to life imprisonment. Her sister Zylpha was released through lack of evidence.

Maria Boyne

Maria Boyne's murder of her husband was committed simply because she could not bear to lose anything she thought of as hers. While she wasn't prepared to part with her lover she had no intention of losing her London home in a divorce either. In her attempt to have it all though, as so many killers had found out before her, she made sure that she lost everything.

Maria's eight-year marriage was over in all but name when she took a knife to her husband. She was already pregnant by her 24-year-old lover, Gary McGinley, and divorce was imminent. The only thing Maria was afraid of was that she might lose her house in the legal battle with her husband. In the weeks before the killing, she told her friends that she just wanted Boyne dead so that she could bring McGinley into her home.

Finally, her murderous intentions were fired up by a particularly vicious argument with her husband. Maria grabbed a knife and brutally stabbed him 31 times, then calmly took a gold chain from around his neck. She would use the money raised from pawning it to celebrate her husband's death with a passionate night in a hotel with McGinley. Boyne's body was found by his elderly father, Michael, who would die soon after giving evidence in the trial. The shock he received on finding his son's bloody corpse meant he too became a victim of Maria's crime.

Maria couldn't evade justice for long, though she was prepared to go to any lengths to do so. In fact, when it became clear that she would face trial for her crime she threw her lover to the wolves, telling the police that it was he who had killed Boyne. No one was fooled. The jury cleared the apparently naive McGinley, but Maria faced the full penalty of the law, damned almost as much by her own lack of remorse and her attempts to shift the blame as by the crime itself. As Judge Paul Worsley, told Maria, "You were motivated by sex and selfishness. You were scheming and devious."

In February 2009, the 30-year-old Maria was found guilty at the Old Bailey, London's central court, murdering Boyne in his bed in April 2008. She was sentenced to life on March 4 and told she would serve a minimum of 24 years in prison. In seeking to serve only her own needs she had killed an innocent man and left two young children, as well as her baby daughter, motherless. In an emotional and touching statement shortly before he died, Boyne's father told the press, "My son thought the world of her despite her numerous affairs. He loved her."

Betty Broderick

After putting so much time, emotional energy, and effort into helping her husband achieve his dreams, to be betrayed at a time when she should have been enjoying the fruits of her labors was a brutal injury for Betty Broderick to suffer. Her life, which had once promised so much, was torn to shreds. The only thing that could satisfy her was the deaths of those who had caused her so much grief.

Betty and Dan Broderick married in April 1969 after meeting at a football game and both shared the same dream: They wanted to be wealthy, secure, and happy—a family that had it all. During the first years of hardship, the couple put everything into their hopes for the future. Dan enrolled in law school, while Betty took jobs to support him. When their four children came along she took sole charge of them, allowing her husband to concentrate on finishing his studies and starting a career. He was offered a job at an established law firm in San Diego, California, and Betty—still determined to do her bit—took a job as a cashier at a restaurant in the evenings.

As the years passed, the Brodericks' dreams of financial security came true. They bought a beautiful house in the affluent Coral Reef suburb of La Jolla in San Diego, became members of exclusive clubs, and took foreign vacations. But along the road to success the shared goals and the loving closeness that had bound them together was lost. Dan became ever more distant from the family. He rarely saw the children and when he and his wife did spend time together it was usually at one of the legal functions or parties that Betty came to detest.

It was at one of these events that Betty overheard a stray comment from her husband that would mark the beginning of her breakdown into emotional chaos. Dan, who was talking to a friend, asked, "Isn't she beautiful?" After a brief moment of delight, Betty soon realized that Dan hadn't been talking about her but Linda Kolkena, a receptionist at the law firm.

Dan now became even more detached from his family than he had been before, and made no secret of his distaste for the woman who had worked so hard to help him climb the ladder of success. On one occasion he told Betty that he was tired of his life and that she was "old, fat, ugly, and boring." Meanwhile, he had taken Linda Kolkena on as his personal assistant.

Betty found out just how calculating her husband could be at the beginning of 1985. Having announced that he was moving the family to a new, bigger, rented house; soon after their belongings were unpacked Dan deserted them and returned to their old home. In a fit of anger and hoping that Dan might realize just how much she had done for him, Betty took all their children and dumped them on him. Her plan, however, backfired badly. Dan hired a housekeeper and finally began to spend more time with his children. Not only did he cope admirably, but his relationship with the children flourished. Betty, meanwhile, was sidelined. His relationship with Linda now openly acknowledged, Dan filed for divorce, and as a top lawyer he was not an easy opponent in a legal battle.

Having lost everything and faced with a long and painful fight, Betty's state of mind began disintegrating. She ignored legal advice, failed to turn up at court hearings, and left a series of telephone messages littered with obscenities and abuse. They would soon come back to haunt her during the divorce proceedings in court. But when she lost custody of the children and Dan took out an injunction preventing her from visiting her old home, something in Betty snapped.

She bought a gun and on November 5, 1988, drove to Dan's home, let herself in with a key she had stolen from her eldest daughter, and made her way to the bedroom. Seeing two shapes beneath the covers of the bed she used to share she shot them both. Dan and Linda were killed instantly.

In court, Betty's defense lawyers claimed that she had been driven to the edge of sanity by the latest developments in the long and bitter divorce battle and had gone to the house to reason with her husband one last time and to commit suicide if she failed to win his sympathy. But while the jury accepted that Betty suffered from psychological disorders they could not help but see the crime as being calculated and premeditated. The prosecution made full use of the hysterical messages Betty had left on her husband's answer phone and, again, they helped paint a picture of a bitter, vindictive woman.

Betty's first trial ended in a hung jury with two jurors preferring a manslaughter verdict rather than murder. At her second hearing, the jury returned a verdict of two counts of second-degree murder, and Betty Broderick was sentenced to two consecutive terms of 15 years to life and two years for the illegal use of a firearm. She was ordered to serve a minimum of 21 years before becoming eligible for parole.

Elizabeth Brown

The tale of the last woman ever to be hanged in Dorset, England, is a sorry one, for Elizabeth Brown's was a true crime of passion, committed in a moment of heartbroken anger. It is also a tale that has left a lasting mark. Her death was watched by a 16-year-old reporter named Thomas Hardy, who would go on to be one of Britain's greatest novelists. Elizabeth's tragic story made such an impression on him that it formed the basis of his greatest novel, *Tess of the D'Urbervilles*.

An attractive redhead, Elizabeth Brown married her husband John later in life than was usual in the mid-19th century. He was 20 years her junior, and it was rumored that he wed only for his wife's money, though the gossip doesn't have the ring of truth to it. Elizabeth was certainly not wealthy; both she and her husband were employed as servants. The couple settled down to married life in the village of Birdsmoorgate, near Beaminster in Dorset, and it soon became obvious that the relationship was not a happy one. Elizabeth became convinced that her youthful husband was unfaithful, and one fateful day in 1856 she was proved right.

Returning home unexpectedly one night, Elizabeth caught her husband beneath the blankets of their marriage bed with another woman. Broken-hearted and humiliated she flew into a rage and a violent quarrel followed. Elizabeth hit out at John who in turn lashed her with a whip. She seized an axe and in the heat of the moment caught him a fatal blow.

Elizabeth then made a mistake that would eventually lead to her own death. Had she told the truth then it is very likely that the circumstances of her husband's death would have been taken into account, and she would have been treated leniently. Instead, the frightened woman told police that her husband's fractured skull had been caused by the kick of a horse. Her story was not believed, she was charged with murder, and went on trial at Dorchester Assizes where she continued to protest her innocence. It did not take a jury long to return a guilty verdict and she was sentenced to death by hanging. Only then did she tell what had really happened.

Although there was a swell of public support for Elizabeth, the Home Secretary refused to grant a reprieve because Elizabeth had lied for so long. She was taken to the scaffold at Dorchester prison on August 9, 1856, and—in a further cruel injustice—delivered into the hands of the infamous hangman William Calcraft, Britain's principal executioner from 1829 to 1874. He was noted for his "short drops," which meant a slow and agonizing death by strangulation rather than a cleanly broken neck.

A crowd of nearly 4,000 people gathered to watch Elizabeth accept her fate with calm and dignity. She had chosen a tight-fitting black silk dress for her execution. The noose was ill-fitting and Elizabeth's death was far from instant. A later report noted what a "fine figure she showed against the sky as she hung in the misty rain," and how "the tight black silk gown set off her shape as she wheeled half round and back" in her death throes. This grisly and salacious report was written by the young Thomas Hardy.

OVERLEAF: The acclaimed English novelist, poet and dramatist, Thomas Hardy who attended the execution of Elizabeth Brown at Dorchester Prison as a young reporter.

BELOW: An illustration from Thomas Hardy's *Tess of the D'Urbervilles*: Elizabeth Brown's tragic story made such an impression on Hardy that it formed the basis of his classic novel.

Ernest Brown

Dorothy Morton's first mistake was to cheat on her husband with Ernest Brown. Her second was to try and end the affair. For her lover had killed before and was determined to keep her by doing so again.

Having begun an affair with one of her husband's employees, a worker on his successful Yorkshire cattle farm, Dorothy Morton soon realized that she had made a terrible misjudgment. Her lover, Ernest Brown, was bad tempered and aggressive. Try as she might, he wouldn't let Dorothy finish the relationship. Instead, he continued to badger her for sex and treat her as if he owned her. On September 5, 1933, Brown found out that Dorothy had been swimming with another man and flew into a terrible rage during which he punched her to the ground. In fear for her life, Dorothy ran from

her lover to the main house and stayed there, waiting for her husband, Frederick, to return. Instead, she heard the sound of a shot outside. Soon after, Brown appeared saying he had killed a rat in the barn. Dorothy waited in vain for her husband. In the early hours of the next morning, she heard an explosion and looked out to see the farm garage on fire. She grabbed her baby and with companion Ann Houseman, ran from the house to report the fire to the police.

When the flames were finally put out, the badly burned body of Frederick Morton was discovered among the cinders. He had been shot in the stomach then he and his two cars were doused with petrol and torched in an attempt to destroy evidence.

Ernest Brown was arrested and charged with murder. He was tried at Leeds Assizes and was soon found guilty. However, as the case had proceeded, it came to light that Brown had also murdered a woman called Evelyn Foster nearly two years earlier. She had offered a lift to a "smartly dressed man" with a bowler hat on January 6, 1931, and he had leaned over to touch her intimately as she drove. When she stopped the car to throw him out, he knocked her unconscious before setting fire to the car with her in it. Burned almost beyond recognition, Evelyn Foster had managed to whisper the man's description to police from her hospital bed before she died, and after Brown's arrest, police realized he was a match. Already sentenced to death it made no sense to try Brown for an earlier crime, but on the day of his execution—February 6, 1934—a chaplain told him, "You should use these last few moments to confess your sins and make your peace with God." As the hangman placed the noose around his neck, Brown murmured "Otterburn," the name of the village where Evelyn had lived.

Albert Burrows

A violent thief who had previously been arrested for horse stealing, cruelty to animals, and assault, when Albert Burrows met Hannah Calladine he added bigamy to the long list of crimes on his charge sheet. It was not, however, the last one he would commit.

Born in Cheadle Hulme, Derbyshire, England, in 1871, by the time World War I broke out, Albert Burrows had amassed an extensive police record. Although he sometimes worked as a laborer on building sites, he was not above raising extra income to take home to his wife and daughter through stealing and his temper had also landed him in trouble on more than one occasion. He was a man who felt that laws and morals just didn't apply to him. So when he began working in an ammunition factory and met a younger woman to whom he was attracted the fact that he already had a wife and child did not stop him starting an affair with her. As far as Hannah was concerned Burrows was a widower whose daughter was being looked after by a housekeeper friend in Glossop and when she fell pregnant in May and Burrows proposed, she accepted. The couple were married in October.

For a short while Burrows was able to secretly support both families, but when the war ended he found himself unemployed and unable to keep up payments. Added to which, Hannah had begun to have suspicions about her husband and wrote a letter to his daughter in Glossop. Burrows first wife was shocked to discover that there was another Mrs Burrows, and her husband was prosecuted, serving six months for bigamy.

Burrows returned to his original wife when he was released, but found that Hannah had obtained a legal order that he financially support her and her infant son, as well. When he couldn't pay up, she had him arrested and he was imprisoned for another three weeks. The situation was no better when he came out the second time. With no job and two families to maintain, Burrows was soon behind on payments again.

The situation grew even worse when Hannah arrived on his doorstep in a cold night just before Christmas in 1919 with his son and Elsie (her daughter from a previous relationship) and demanded to be taken in. With his outraged wife protesting, Burrows allowed Hannah to stay, saying that she couldn't be turned away on such a night—his wife walked out the following day. Hannah ended up staying the final three weeks of her life with her former husband.

On January 12, 1920, Burrows again appeared in court, but this time he had solved his problems. He told the justices that Hannah had found a good job and left taking the children with her. Mrs Burrows returned to the family home soon after. Finally, it seemed that Albert Burrows had put the stresses and strains of supporting two families behind him. The true extent of his crimes, however, would later come to light in the most appalling way.

On March 4, 1923, a four-year-old boy named Thomas Wood went missing after having been seen with Burrows. He was quickly taken into custody and under police questioning broke down. The truth that was to be unravelled made his previous crimes look like minor misdemeanors. Burrows admitted that he had sexually assaulted the small boy, then dropped him down a mine shaft. When it was searched, little Thomas's body was indeed found, and alongside were the remains of Hannah Calladine and her two children, Albert, and Elsie.

The trial of Albert Edward Burrows for the murder of Hannah Calladine, 32, and her fifteen-month-old son was held at the Derbyshire Assizes and began on July 8, 1923. The horrified jury took less than a quarter of an hour to bring in a verdict of guilty. With the death sentence already passed, the authorities didn't waste any time bringing the cases for Elsie or Thomas Wood to court and Burrows paid for his crimes at Bagthorpe Gaol in Nottingham on the August 8, 1923 with a noose around his neck.

William Burton

A cheat and a liar, William Burton, made sweeping promises in order to seduce the young woman who had caught his eye. He had no intention of keeping them though, and when he found out that she was pregnant the cold-hearted Burton decided she had become a problem.

As a 29-year-old rabbit catcher at Manor Farm in the Dorset village of Gussage Saint Michael, William Burton was no great catch himself, though he possessed a certain amount of charm. It had won him a respectable wife, who worked as a schoolteacher, and the couple had recently welcomed a baby to their flat above the village post office. Burton was dissatisfied though. His wife was somewhat older than him and now a mother. His passion for her was waning, just as it was growing for another woman.

At Manor Farm there was a beautiful young cook named Winifred Mary Mitchell. Burton became determined to have her. He gave her the full benefit of his rough charm, but she was not the type of woman to give her love easily. For two months he tried to seduce her, and still she resisted, knowing that he was married man with a young child.

Winifred was finally won over when Burton promised to take her to Canada where they could begin a new life together. Convinced that Burton loved her enough to leave his family behind, Winifred's reluctance was cast aside. Burton's promises were empty. What had started for him as a challenge and then an enjoyable sexual liaison abruptly became a liability when Winifred fell pregnant. He could see only one solution that didn't involve the inconvenience of either making good on his promises or having his cheating brought to light with the birth of an illegitimate child.

On March 29, 1913, Burton again promised Winifred that they would soon run away together and arranged to meet her in a secluded spot. He then borrowed a gun, saying he needed it to kill a cat. When his lover arrived for their illicit tryst, he shot her and buried her body in a shallow grave.

Unfortunately for him, on May 2, the corpse was discovered, and when police discovered scraps of passionate letters Burton had written to Winifred, he was arrested. William Burton was found guilty of murder and became the last man ever to be hanged at Dorchester Prison on June 21, 1913.

ABOVE: An aerial view of Dorchester prison, William Burton was the last man to be hanged there.

Kitty Byron

The law is supposed to stand apart from public opinion, but in Kitty Byron's case her conviction for murder was followed by such an outcry that the Home Secretary himself stepped in, saving her first from the gallows and later allowing Kitty's release from prison after she served just six years of a life sentence.

Kitty Byron's was a woeful tale. She had the misfortune to fall in love with Arthur Reginald Baker. In public, Baker seemed to be respectable married man and was a member of the London Stock Exchange. However, in private Baker was a heavy drinker and prone to outbursts of violent temper, during which he often attacked his mistress. On one occasion he almost strangled her.

Baker lived a double life, with his wife in one home while Kitty was set up in lodgings on Duke Street in the West End of London. As far as the landlady was concerned the couple were Mr and Mrs Baker and unremarkable except for their furious arguments, which often ended in violence. On the evening of November 7, 1902, there was a particularly vicious quarrel that ended with Kitty appearing on the landing in her nightdress to avoid her lover's fists. The next morning, tired of the fighting, the landlady gave them two months' notice to leave.

The relationship calm down for a while after the incident, but it seems that Baker was growing bored of his mistress. After taking Kitty a cup of tea before leaving for work one morning, he took the landlady to one side and confessed she was not his wife, but a girl of "no class." He assured her that he would make sure Kitty left the premises the very next day.

Unfortunately for Baker, a housemaid overheard the conversation. The news, which she quickly passed on to Kitty, would cost him his life. On hearing how her abusive lover now planned to coldly abandon her and have her thrown out of her home, Kitty uttered the words that would come back to haunt her at her trial. Baker would die, she said, "before the day is out."

The landlady was mystified. Why, she asked, did Kitty stay with a violent, drunken bully if they were not married? Kitty's reply was short and simple: "Because I love him," she said, before going out to buy a sharp knife. She then sent a note via a post office messenger boy to Baker at his office. It read, "Want you importantly. Kitty."

Baker came at once, following the boy back to the post office where Kitty was waiting. As he approached the woman he had beaten so often she pulled the knife from where it was hidden in her muff and stabbed Baker twice.

Her trial began in December 1902 and Kitty's was a pathetic figure as she stood weeping in the dock. While admitting that she had killed Baker, she said that she did not know what she was doing and pleaded not guilty to murder. Public sympathy was with her, but the judge's less so. While the defense pleaded manslaughter, he did not agree and summed up in favor of a murder verdict though with a strong recommendation that the court should be merciful. But clemency was not forthcoming: Kitty was found guilty of murder and sentenced to death.

However, her fortunes were about to take a dramatic turn for the better. The trial had been widely reported in the press, and the public mood was that the sentence was far too harsh considering how Kitty had suffered at Baker's hands. While she awaited the gallows, a petition was circulated and 15,000 signatures collected before it was handed to the Home Secretary. It included the names of clerks who had worked with Baker in the City and knew exactly the type of man he was. A reprieve was duly granted, and Kitty's sentence reduced to life imprisonment. In 1907 it was reduced again and she was released from prison in 1908.

Frederick Bywaters

Percy Thompson was the victim of a classic crime of passion. In refusing to divorce his wife, Edith, so that she and the man she adored could be together, he brought the anger of both down upon his head. But while the lovers both eventually hanged for his murder, it is likely that only one of them was guilty.

In 1916, Percy Thompson married Edith Graydon. He was 21 and she was just 18, and the couple settled down to their life together in Ilford, Essex, England. Percy was a clerk at the Pacific and Orient shipping line, and Edith was a bookkeeper at a millinery firm. For almost six years, they enjoyed a life of quiet domesticity, but that was before Edith was swept away by a passion that she had never imagined possible.

In the summer of 1921, the Thompsons joined a group for a holiday visit to the Isle of Wight. Among the party was 19-year-old Frederick Bywaters, a shipping line employee and a confident young man

ABOVE: Frederick Bywaters, seated, at the inquest into the death of Percy Thompson.

Bywaters moved in. But such was his love for Edith that Bywaters could not be satisfied with the role of lover. Although the affair was made easy by the fact that he lived under the same roof as his mistress, he could not bear to watch her pretending to still be a dutiful wife. Before long, he confessed to Thompson that he and Edith were deeply in love and asked him to divorce her so that she would be free to marry again. Thompson was understandably furious. A huge argument erupted and Bywaters was thrown out of the house. Edith was told that her affair was at and end.

Nevertheless, the lovers continued to see each other whenever it could be contrived and, when they couldn't meet, sent each other long, passionate letters. In September 1922, Bywaters' ship docked in England. On the afternoon of October 3, he and Edith had a secret rendezvous in a London teashop. Later that night she and her husband went to the theater and returned late to Ilford. As they walked home an assailant leaped from the darkness. It was Bywaters.

As the young man repeatedly plunged a knife into Percy, Edith screamed and cried for help, pleading with her lover, "Oh don't, oh don't!" Her reaction was, said witnesses at her trial, one of genuine horror. She also pleaded with a doctor who rushed to the scene to save her husband's life. However, she did not tell the police that she knew the attacker though the thin protection this brought Bywaters soon failed. After talking to neighbors and discovering the stack of letters Edith had received from her lover, a motive for murder was established. Edith and Bywaters were arrested.

At their trial, the prosecution alleged that the murder had been planned that afternoon at the teashop rendezvous. Bywaters denied it and told the jury that he had tried to reason with Thompson again and ask him to divorce Edith, and in the ensuing an argument Thompson had threatened to shoot him. He insisted that he had acted in self-defense and even so had only meant to injure, not kill.

with a strong personality. The mutual attraction between him and Edith Thompson was explosive. Before the short vacation was over, Edith confided to her sister that she no longer loved her husband.

Overwhelmed by her feelings for Bywaters, Edith set out to persuade her husband to allow him to become a lodger at their home, telling him that the extra money would be useful. Reluctantly, Thompson agreed, and

However, the couple were betrayed by their own letters. When the prosecution produced 62 of them, sent from Edith to Bywaters, they painted a damning picture of adulterous lovers plotting to kill the man who stood between them. In each, Edith referred to her lover by his pet name "Darlint" and many told how she was trying to kill her husband by putting glass into his food, "Big pieces too, not powdered." She also wrote of trying to poison Thompson: "He puts great stress on the tea tasting bitter." And more: "I am going to try the glass again when it is safe." In one particularly passionate letter Edith wrote, "This thing that I am going to do for both of us—will it ever, at all, make any difference darlint? Do you understand what I mean? Will you ever think any the less of me?"

In response, Bywaters told the court there never had been a real plot to murder Thompson. The letters were just the fantasies of two people who adored each other but were forced apart. The letters also contained references to an abortion that Edith had had when she found she was carrying Bywaters' baby and it is interesting to note that such was the morality of the time that the ignorant jurors interpreted many of the phrases in the letter referring to the terminated pregnancy as being further death threats. Edith's defense counsel, however, made no attempt to clear up the jurors' misunderstandings. He feared that the knowledge that she had not only cheated on her husband but aborted her lover's child would lose the jury's sympathy completely.

The case against the lovers was strong, yet there was one thing in Edith's favor. A single hard fact that the defense case finally rested upon. The pathologist's report stated that no glass or traces of poison had been found in the body of Percy Thompson.

There was to be no mercy, however. The judge—Mr Justice Shearman—took pleasure in detailing Edith's "wicked affection" for her lover in his summing up, saying, "This is a squalid and rather indecent case of lust and adultery." The jury took two hours to consider their verdicts. Edith Thompson and Frederick Bywaters were pronounced guilty and the judge sentenced them to hang. They died on the gallows on the morning of January 9, 1923.

To the end, Bywaters remained both dignified and determined to protect the reputation of his beloved Edith. From his condemned cell, he wrote in her defence, saying "For her to be hanged as a criminal is too awful. She didn't commit the murder. I did. She never planned it, she never knew about it. She is innocent, absolutely innocent."

BELOW: Crowds lining up outside the Old Bailey, London, during the trial of Edith Thompson and her lover, Frederick Bywaters, for the murder of her husband.

Cheryl Crane

Over the years Hollywood has been the scene of many murders, some every bit as dramatic as those on-screen. But there have been few stranger cases than the slaying of gangster Johnny Stompanato by the 14-year-old daughter of movie star Lana Turner.

As has often been the case with Hollywood folk, while Lana Turner enjoyed a thriving career in the movies her private life was much less successful. It was while she was coming to terms with the collapse of her most recent marriage that she received a telephone call that would end in death, and a murder trial for Lana's young daughter, Cheryl Crane. At the end of the line

RIGHT: Cheryl Crane, daughter of actor Lana Turner, sits in a chair at the time of her trial for the murder of gangster Johnny Stompanato.

BELOW: American actor Lana Turner (center), wearing dark sunglasses, sitting next to her ex-husband, Stephen Crane, in a courtroom during the murder trial of their daughter, Cheryl Crane.

was a man, a complete stranger, who told the star that they had mutual friends and asked her out on a blind date. Showing an incredible lack of judgement, Lana agreed and so began a torrid relationship with local criminal Johnny Stompanato.

An ex-U.S. Marine, con-man, and associate of known gangsters, Stompanato was a smooth talker who soon insinuated himself into Lana's bed, her Los Angeles mansion, and her bank account. And once he was firmly installed in her life things quickly turned sour. Stompanato bullied and abused his famous lover and gambled her money away. Lana's daughter Cheryl regularly begged her mother to end the relationship, but Lana replied, "I'm too afraid." As a court would later hear, Stompanato was an associate of big-time gangsters Bugsy Siegel and Mickey Cohen, and had

ABOVE: High-angle view of American actor Lana Turner (right) seated in a courtroom, surrounded by reporters during the trial of her daughter, Cheryl Crane.

already told Lana what would happen if she tried to leave him, threatening, "I'll mutilate you. I will hurt you so you'll be so repulsive that you'll have to hide forever." On another occasion he told her, "When I say hop, you hop. When I say jump, you jump."

Such threats became ever more frequent and on the night of April 4, 1958, Stompanato and Lana had a violet argument during which he again threatened to scar her, shouting, "I'll get you if it takes a day, a week, a month or a year. If I can't do it myself, I'll get someone who will. That's my business."

Outside the door Cheryl was listening. In fear for her mother's life and driven to a frenzy of hatred by the gangster's threats, she fetched a long-bladed kitchen knife, ran into the room, thrust it into Stompanato's stomach, and killed him.

As might be expected for a case involving such a high-profile celebrity, the ensuing inquest was a sensational. On live television, audiences greater than any she had received before watched Lana Turner give an account of the events leading up to Stompanato's death and a passionate defense of her daughter. As a minor, Cheryl did not appear in court, but gave evidence in writing. Her statement read: "They had an argument and he was threatening Mother. He said he would kill her and hurt Daddy, Grandma, and me. He said he had ways of doing it. My mother was very frightened. I went down to the kitchen and got the knife. I took the knife up to the room in case he hurt mother. I rushed into the room and stuck him with the knife. He screamed."

The jury returned a verdict of justifiable homicide, effectively clearing Cheryl of blame for the killing. On hearing it, a friend of Stompanato leaped up in the public gallery and shouted, "It's lies, all lies. The girl was in love with him as well. He was killed because of jealousy between mother and daughter." Cheryl was released from a juvenile prison to resume normal life with her movie star mother. The scandal had no ill-effects on Lana's career. In fact, she earned an $2 million from her next film, *Imitation of Life*—an incredible fee at the time. She needed the money: Stompanato's family sued her and received an undisclosed settlement.

Dr. Hawley Harvey Crippen

The case of Dr Crippen is one of the most famous in the history of crime. Involving a nagging, unfaithful wife, a sexually charged affair, a desperate escape, and grisly remains found in a basement, Crippen's tale contains all the ingredients of a thriller novel.

Crippen was an American doctor, who worked as a consultant ear specialist in England despite not being qualified to practice medicine outside of the United States. Flamboyant and dressy, he was charming in public but hid his private turmoil. All was not happy in the Crippen household.

Following the death of his first wife, Crippen had married again in 1892 at the age of 31, to a young woman of 19 named Cora. They had a complicated courtship. At the time, Cora was already the mistress of a stove manufacturer who paid for the singing lessons that would eventually propel her onto the London music hall stage under the name Belle Elmore. While she eventually agreed to be Crippen's wife, marriage did nothing to settle Cora. She liked to be center stage; to be adored and admired. Like many others of the same temperament, she tried to satisfy her need for attention in the arms of numerous men. Her string of lovers included an ex-boxer and several of the lodgers who took rooms with the Crippens. Meanwhile, she grew contemptuous of her husband and her bad temper often spilled over into nagging and arguments.

So, when Crippen met a 17-year-old Polish typist named Ethel Le Neve and was attracted to her, he felt no guilt. After all, he knew that Cora had affairs and made his life a misery. He hired Ethel as his bookkeeper and—surprisingly—the pair remained on professional, terms for seven years before becoming lovers.

It was Cora's vicious tongue that sealed her fate. When Ethel fell pregnant and had a miscarriage, Cora was quick to humiliate her husband, claiming to her music hall friends that the baby could have been fathered by any one of a number of men that Ethel had been sleeping with. Such accusations were rich, coming from a woman who delighted in her many affairs, and drove Crippen into a rage. Cora, he decided, had to die.

Crippen's chose poison as the cleanest murder method and accordingly gave his wife a strong dose in a nightcap on January 31, 1910. But when that didn't have the required effect he simply shot Cora in the back of the head, then dismembered her body and buried it in the cellar, covering the parts in quicklime to help them decompose more quickly. To cover his tracks he then told her friends that she had rushed to the bedside of a sick relative in the United States. As time passed and she didn't return, he said that she had become seriously ill, and then that she had died. Nevertheless, Cora's friends were suspicious. They alerted the police who questioned Crippen and searched the house. Although on that occasion they found nothing, Crippen was spooked, and decided to flee.

Together with Ethel, who was disguised as a boy, Crippen boarded the SS *Montrose*, which was bound for his homeland. But back in London the police returned and, finding the house deserted, this time searched more thoroughly. Before the ship left harbor, the tale of the grisly remains found in the coal cellar were splashed all over the newspapers along with Crippen's photo. And as the boat steamed out toward America, a copy caught the eye of the captain of the SS Montrose. Recognizing one of his passengers, he famously sent a message to shore, which read: "Have strong suspicion that

BELOW: A photograph of Dr. Crippen from 1910, the year he is alleged to have poisoned his wife and dismembered he body before fleeing across the Atlantic Ocean.

Crippen London cellar murder and accomplice are among saloon passengers." Crippen became the first murderer to be caught by wireless telegraph.

At the trial, Crippen gallantly played down Ethel's involvement in his wife's death, and she was acquitted of murder. Crippen also pleaded innocent, saying the remains found at the house on Hilldrop Crescent were not those of his wife, but the jury did not believe him. he was found guilty of murder and hanged on November 23, 1910.

However, it appears Crippen did not kill his wife after all. In 2007, DNA analysis of the body in Crippen's cellar suggested that the body was not Cora's. Instead the murder victim was an unknown man!

OVERLEAF: 39 Hilltop Crescent, London: The house where Dr Crippen was alleged to have murdered his second wife Belle Elmore.

BELOW: A detective leads Doctor Hawley Harvey Crippen from the SS *Megantic*, upon arrival in England, in August 1910.

Dr. Philip Cross

For some men entering the twilight of their lives, a new passion with a much younger woman is a chance to turn the clock back to a time when they were young and vigorous. Such infatuations can be so all-consuming that they become deadly.

Dr. Philip Cross had long preferred women who had a fresh glow of youth about them. When he married at the age of 44, his wife Laura was just 22. For 18 years, the couple lived comfortably and happily at Shandy Hall in the village of Dripsey, County Cork, Ireland. Dr Cross's practice was successful, and over the years the couple were blessed with six children. However, the contentment of the Cross family home came to an abrupt end when Laura took on a new governess for the children.

Effie Skinner was just 20, by then more than 40 years younger than Cross, and not strikingly pretty. Nevertheless, she had a youthful charm that immediately attracted Cross. Soon he had become totally besotted. Although the strength of his lust threatened to overwhelm him, Cross tried to suppress the emotion, but one day as Effie stood before him reporting on the children's' progress he could contain himself no longer. He leaned over and kissed her.

Cross regretted it immediately, fearing that the

shocked and unresponsive Effie might tell his wife or—even worse—that she might leave. Effie had no wish to give up a comfortable job though, and stayed quiet. But the longer she was in the house, the more intense became Cross's lust until it became so obvious that Mrs Cross could not help but notice. She immediately sacked Effie even though she protested that any sexual inclination was all on the doctor's side.

The governess left for Dublin and was pursued there by Cross. Now, at last, away from his wife's watchful eyes he allowed his passion free reign. Effie succumbed to his advances. It seems that finally having the object of his lust robbed Dr Cross of what remained of his senses, for he was now determined that she must become his wife, and mistress of Shandy Hall, whatever the cost. And the price that must be paid to satisfy his passion was Laura Cross's life.

It was easy for the doctor to arrange his wife's death. Having procured a good supply of arsenic, which he said was to be used for sheep dip, he began to poison her. As she grew unwell, the doctor reassured her that it was not a serious illness and gave her a remedy that contained yet more arsenic. Within a month she was dead. And within two weeks of that, Philip Cross was married to Effie Skinner.

Had he not been so quick to wed his mistress, Cross may never have been discovered, but Laura's friends and family were already suspicious about her death. She had always been a healthy, robust woman and never displayed any of the symptoms of the heart problems that Cross had said killed her. Although he tried to keep his new marriage secret, when he brought Effie back to Shandy Hall it couldn't be hidden for long. Suspicions became accusations, and the police exhumed Laura's body. A postmortem found no sign of heart disease, but plenty of arsenic and strychnine. Dr Philip Cross went on trial for murder at the Munster Assizes in Cork and was found guilty on December 18, 1887.

George Crossman

George Crossman's were not really crimes of passion in the true sense, yet the murders he committed are worth mentioning here because they were all in the name of love. A serial womanizer and bigamist, he married seven women—that we know of—and one by one he killed them.

At the age of 32, George Crossman was married to his fifth wife. His first three marriages had all been legitimate, but this was his second wedding conducted under a false name. Wife number five was a widowed nurse called Ellen Sampson. After her joyous wedding day in January 1903, she returned with her husband to her new home in Ladysmith Road, Kensal Rise, north London, without the slightest suspicion that it was already the home of wife number four, Edith. As soon as their wedding night was over Ellen became surplus to requirements. Crossman smashed her over the head and hid her body in a trunk in the attic. By the time Edith returned home from visiting friends everything in the house was normal. She would never know that her husband had found time for a bigamous marriage

and a murder while she was away.

Incredibly Crossman and Edith lived a fairly happy married life for the next two years, though that certainly would not have been the case if she had known the truth: she was not legally married (there was yet another wife in the background), there was a body rotting in a trunk at the top of the house; and during that time Crossman married wives six and seven during trips away from home.

It was only when the couple's lodger William Dell started to complain about the awful smell coming from one of the upstairs room that Crossman's murdering secret was revealed. In March 1904, Crossman hastily tried to get the trunk out of the house, but it was too late. By then William Dell had already alerted police about what he strongly suspected was the smell of a rotting body, and Crossman was caught in the act or trying to remove the trunk on March 23. He managed to dash past the police, who gave chase. The certain knowledge that he was going to die a painful death on the gallows was too much for Crossman. After running almost a mile, he stopped to cut his own throat from ear to ear with a razor.

Sir John Henry Delves Broughton

The murder of a known womanizer in Kenya will probably never now be solved, but the prime suspect remains Sir Henry Delves Broughton. However, though he stood trial for the killing, with the help of his young wife—whose lover was the victim—Sir Henry was found not guilty of killing his rival.

Kenya's **White Highlands** were once nicknamed "Happy Valley" due to the excessive drink, drugs, and sex parties enjoyed by its wealthy inhabitants in the days when Kenya was still a colony of the British Empire. Foremost among the hedonists was Josslyn Victor Hay, 22nd Earl of Erroll and Baron Kilmarnock. Locally, he was known as "The Passionate Peer," for the 39-year-old aristocrat was a sophisticated, handsome, sexual predator; an accomplished seducer, whose favorite line was, "To hell with husbands."

On November 30, 1940, Hay was drinking at the Muthaiga Club, a watering hole favored by the wealthy British, when two recently arrived strangers entered. Sir John Henry "Jock" Delves Broughton was a property magnate and racing fanatic in his late 50s and on his arm was an ash-blonde beauty—26-year-old Diana Caldwell whom Sir Henry had married only weeks before the pair had emigrated to Kenya. Hay later told friends, "Never can I remember a woman having such an immediate impact on me. I saw her eyes boring into me and I knew then that I must have her. I walked over to her while Jock was at the bar and said to her, Well, who is going to tell Jock—you or I?'"

It did not take long for Hay to seduce the beautiful young bride. On January 18, 1941, Diana confessed to her husband that she had fallen madly in love, and reminded him of an extraordinary pact that Sir Henry had made with her before they were married. Aware of the great differences in their ages, Sir Henry had promised that if Diana ever fell in love with a younger man he would provide her with a quick divorce and several thousand pounds a year afterward. He had never expected the marriage to come to an end so quickly though. Instead of immediately honoring his promise, he asked his wife to take a three-month trip with him to Ceylon and told her that if she would just promise to reconsider then she could even bring Hay along.

Diana considered the generous offer for a couple of days and then rejected it. She walked out on Sir Henry, telling him that she was going to live with Hay.

Three days later, Sir Henry called the police to report a break-in. Two revolvers, some money, and a cigarette case had been stolen. The same day he saw his lawyers about a divorce and later wrote the following words to a friend: "They say they are in love with each other and mean to get married. It is a hopeless position and I'm going to cut my losses. I think I'll go to Ceylon. There's nothing for me to live in Kenya for."

At 3am on January 24, 1941, a truck driver discovered Hay's body slumped under the dashboard of his car, which had left the road and plunged into a ditch only three miles from Sir Henry's home. He had been shot through the head at point-blank range with a .32 caliber revolver.

Strangely, the police didn't announce that they were treating it as a murder case until January 25, by which time the body had already been buried. But once they

RIGHT: Sir John Henry "Jock" Delves Broughton, pictured at the first day of York races in England in 1937.

did, Diana quickly came forward and accused her husband of cold-bloodedly killing her lover out of jealousy. Sir Henry was taken into custody. In another odd turn of events, however, Diana relented almost immediately. By the time police formally charged Sir Henry with the murder, she had flown to Johannesburg to hire top criminal lawyer Harry Morris to defend her husband. It was to be a worthwhile investment.

Morris called experts to prove that the three bullets fired at Hay could not have come from any gun owned by Sir Henry. The accused also performed masterfully in the dock, at one point saying, "She could ask who she liked. I should not have tried to stop her in any event. I see no point in it. We met every day at the club and I cannot see it makes any difference if a man comes to stay the night. In my experience of life, if you try to stop a woman doing anything, she wants to do it all the more. With a young wife the only thing to do is keep her amused." What motive, it was asked, could a man so coolly accepting of his wife's infidelity have in murdering her lover?

On July 1, 1941, Sir Henry Delves Broughton was found not guilty of murdering Josslyn Hay. The file on the crime has never been closed, and the murderer has never been caught. Sir Henry committed suicide in Liverpool on December 5, 1942, leaving a note that said he had found the strain of the trial and publicity too much to bear. Diana returned to Kenya where she remained until her death in 1987, a rich, enigmatic, extravagant lady to the last.

Geza de Kaplany

Most men who marry a beautiful and glamorous young wife celebrate their good luck in winning a woman that so many other men desire. But for Geza de Kaplany, his wife's good looks were a reason for jealousy and suspicion. When he was struck by impotence and could no longer make love to her, he found a solution to his problems: if he couldn't have her, then he would make sure that no one else wanted her.

Born in Hungary in 1926, Geza de Kaplany was working in a hospital in San Jose, California, when he met 25-year-old Hanja. She was 10 years his junior, a glamor model and ex-showgirl who had her choice of men, but the doctor's own good looks attracted her and she fell in love. He, in turn, was smitten by the lovely young creature and soon the couple were joined in marriage. Less than a month later, Hanja was brutally and fatally mutilated by her husband.

It began with an obsession that other men in their apartment building were pursuing the eager Hanja, but de Kaplany's unravelling mental state also meant that he could no longer sustain an erection. Sunk in black thoughts and comparing his own inadequacy to his gorgeous young wife's obvious sexual allure, he came to an insane conclusion: Hanja must be made ugly.

On the evening of August 28, 1962, loud classical music flooded the Ranchero Palms Apartments in San Jose, accompanied by equally loud blood-chilling screams. Neighbors quickly called the police, but by the time they arrived it was already too late. Hanja was found tied to her bed. De Kaplany had poured sulfuric and nitric acids over his wife, and mutilated her with a knife. She suffered third degree corrosive burns over 60 per cent of her body with most of the brutality focussed on her genitals. So bad was the damage that one of the ambulance crew had to be treated for burns sustained simply by touching her skin. Maimed beyond comprehension, still Hajna de Kaplany fought for her life. It proved to be a losing battle. After 33 days in hospital, she succumbed to her injuries.

De Kaplany told police that Hajna had been unfaithful to him, and that he had just wanted to destroy her beauty rather than kill her. Somewhere in his twisted mind he was aware of the horror of his crime: When he saw police photographs of his wife protest and accusations that gruesome postmortem photographs of Hajna de Kaplany had been removed from his file prior to review by the California State Parole Board. After working in Taiwan as a medical missionary he broke parole conditions and got a job at a hospital in Munich in 1980. However, when his past became known he was swiftly fired. Incredibly, he found another woman willing to be his wife and became a naturalized German citizen in order to avoid extradition back to America.

ABOVE: Dr. Geza de Kaplany, who tortured his wife with acid on her face and knife wounds to much of her body.

BELOW: Hajna de Kaplany, pictured in her showgirl days. Her beauty, combined with her husbands insane jealousy, led to her horrific death.

wounds he broke down. At his trial in 1963, de Kaplany pleaded not guilty to his wife's murder on the grounds of insanity. He claimed to suffer from multiple-personality disorder and said that the sadistic crime was not committed by him but by his alter ego, Pierre de la Roche. Nevertheless, de Kaplany was convicted of first degree murder, though due to his irrational behavior before and during the trial he was sentenced to life imprisonment rather than death.

De Kaplany actually served less than 12 years for his insane and deadly attack. He was released in 1975 amid

Nannie Hazle Doss

What drove Nannie to kill was not love and passion, but the lack of it. As hard as she tried to find a husband who would match up to the dashing men in the bodice-ripping books and true romance magazines she had become addicted to, none of them ever did. And to make way for the next unlucky husband, one by one they had to die.

Nannie Hazle Doss—who also became known as "Arsenic Annie," the "Jolly Black Widow," and the "Giggling Grandma"—was a cuddly creature with twinkling eyes and a wide smile by the time she finally stood trial for her crimes. Beneath the sweet exterior was a woman who killed without a second thought. She had been born Nancy Hazle, in 1905 in Blue

RIGHT: Nannie Doss pictured with her grandchildren, in a courthouse corridor during a hearing to decide her fate for the death of her husband, Samuel Doss.

BELOW: Nannie Doss looks happy and relaxed as she talks with homicide detective Captain Harry Stege before her arraignment on a charge of murder.

Mountain, Alabama, and, in a similar tale to many women who turned murderer, led a miserable childhood. Beaten cruelly and forced to work on the family farm by a father who may also have sexually abused her, Nancy—now known to all as Nannie—escaped her hellish home at the age of 15 by marrying a man named Charlie Braggs who she had met only four months previously.

The marriage was doomed from the start. Braggs insisted that his mother come live with the newlyweds in Tulsa, Oklahoma, and before long started staying away from home for nights at a time while he played around with other women. Meanwhile Nannie was swamped with children—the couple had four daughters in four years—and having failed to find the love for which she had always yearned, turned to drink and lost herself in romance magazines.

Nevertheless, as it turned out Braggs was the most fortunate of her five husbands, though the same can't be said for two of the children. He returned home one day in the spring of 1927 to find them dying on the floor (they were later alleged to have been Nannie's first victims) and he walked out, taking the surviving oldest child and leaving his wife with the youngest. He later said that he had left, "because I was frightened of what she would do." His instinct probably saved his life. Braggs filed for divorce and it was finalized the next year, by which time Nannie had already lined up husband number two.

This one didn't last long. He failed to satisfy and within a year of the marriage Frank Harelson died of stomach trouble. Husband number three must have come closer to fulfiling Nannie's fantasies because he survived until 1952 before the same death took him, too. Number four, Richard Morton, left a healthy insurance policy, and by now Nannie had hit her stride and felt that she no longer needed to confine herself to husbands. In short order, Nannie's mother, her two sisters, and the nephew of one of her deceased husbands were added to the list of mysterious deaths.

It was only upon the death in 1954 of Nannie's fifth husband, Samuel Doss, that an autopsy was ordered. It was discovered that there was enough arsenic in him to kill 20 men. Arrested, she chuckled and giggled through police interrogation, not appearing to understand the gravity of her crimes. She was still smiling when, at her trial, the court was told that her estimated tally of victims was 11. Nannie Doss showed neither regret nor remorse and calmly explained that she had poisoned the last four of her five husbands because they were, "dullards." None of them had lived up to the glamorous fictional men in her paperbacks and magazines. She was sentenced to life imprisonment and died in prison of leukaemia in 1965.

BELOW: Nannie Doss, pictured in a mug-shot taken in Tulsa, Oklahoma in October 1954.

Ruth Ellis

Since immortalized in literature and film, the tale of the last woman in Britain to be hanged is one of tangled relationships and immorality set in the murky world of sleazy London nightclubs. It is also a warning. When someone allows their life to slide into depravity, the results can be disastrous.

Ruth Ellis began life as Ruth Hornby in the Welsh seaside town of Rhyl. Born on October 9, 1926, as she grew up her one ambition was to get out of the stifling town and away from her unhappy childhood home. By the age of 17, she was working in a factory in London during the war years and had met a Canadian serviceman. He took the opportunity of being on the opposite side of the Atlantic from his wife

OVERLEAF (LEFT): Ruth Ellis, in a photograph probably taken in the flat above her club on the Brompton Road in Knightsbridge, London.

OVERLEAF (RIGHT): The Magdela public house in London where Ruth Ellis shot her husband David Blakey.

BELOW: Ruth Ellis posing in stockings and suspenders, in a picture taken by a Captain Ritchie in 1954.

and children to have an affair with the pretty young teenager and showered Ruth with gifts while escorting her around London's nightspots. Sadly, his passion waned when he found out that his young lover was pregnant. Like many girls of her day, Ruth was literally left holding the baby when the war ended and her boyfriend returned to his family.

Devastated, Ruth declared that she would never trust or love a man again and persuaded her mother to take care of her infant son. Then she returned to London to seek work. One particular advert caught her eye, it read, "Wanted. Model for Camera Club. Nude but artistic poses. No experience necessary." Ruth attended an interview, stripped off her clothes, and was awarded a job posing for photographers who rarely bothered to fill their cameras with film. She also happily escorted the men who paid to look at her naked out to dine and dance in London's West End.

It wasn't long before Ruth forgot her pledge not to become involved with men and she took up with another who saw her as an easy target. Morris Conley owned the sleazy Court Club, had served time for fraud and illegal gambling, and employed women who would satisfy all needs of his customers. Ruth soon became an employee and quickly mastered the art of flirting with the men who came to the club and tricking them into buying fake Champagne and overpriced food. For her troubles, Ruth received a ten percent commission on top of her five pounds a week wage. However, there was even more money to be made by allowing customers to purchase her body as well, and Ruth proved herself a willing and able prostitute. As one client later reported, "She was an artist. She gave you the full treatment and by the time she had finished you felt on top of the world." At the same time she was also sleeping with Conley who felt he had the right to sex with his hostess employees. They were rewarded for complying with gifts of beautiful gowns, and should they refuse the dresses were slashed, and the girls fired.

At the age of 23, Ruth fell pregnant again, but this time opted for a dangerous backstreet abortion. Within a year, she was married to 41-year-old divorced dentist George Ellis and pregnant again, though there was no guarantee that the child was her new husband's. Nevertheless, Ruth decided to keep the baby and her daughter was duly placed in the care of her mother while Ruth and George continued to live a decadent lifestyle in London's seedier hangouts. The marriage wasn't destined to last though. Ruth's husband was an alcoholic with a violent temper, and the couple were constantly separating and reuniting as passion and possessiveness alternated between contempt and hatred between them. Eventually, George used doubts over their daughter's paternity as an excuse to desert his wife. By 1951 they were divorced.

With George's financial support withdrawn, Ruth returned to her job at the Court Club, which by now had become the Carroll Club, though the activities within its walls hadn't changed in the slightest. Ruth's enthusiasm for her work was rewarded with a rent-free, two-bedroom Mayfair apartment supplied by Conley while her expertise as a prostitute brought numerous gifts from clients. One admirer bought her a race horse, Ruth's wardrobe was filled with expensive designer clothes, and her purse with bundles of banknotes given to her by rich, international businessmen. She now counted celebrities among her friends including the World Champion racing driver Mike Hawthorn, who introduced Ruth to the man that would end her life.

David Blakely was engaged to another girl when he took up with Ruth. Three years younger than her, he followed a by now well-established pattern in Ruth's lovers, turning violent and abusive when drunk. But unlike previous boyfriends he had had a decent education at a public school, and when sober had excellent manners and treated her with more respect than most other Carroll Club customers. For once Ruth was sleeping with a man because she wanted to, rather than because he was just part of the job. When she became pregnant again in 1953, Blakely seemed ready to take responsibility. As Ruth would later recall, "David was very concerned about my welfare. Although he was engaged to another girl, he offered to marry me and he said it seemed unnecessary for me to get rid of the child, but I did not want to take advantage of him. I was not really in love with him at the time and it was quite unnecessary to marry me. I thought I could get out of the mess quite easily. In fact, I did so with the abortion."

After the latest pregnancy was terminated, Ruth's

affections for Blakely waned and she began seeing other men without his knowledge. Among them was company director Desmond Cussen whose help she began to rely on. Due to Blakely's jealousy and suspicions about her activities, Ruth had not been able to entertain clients at the Carroll Club and had subsequently lost her job. Cussen set her up in a flat and became a frequent visitor. Nevertheless, she was still sleeping with Blakely and their relationship had become increasingly stormy, swinging from warm embraces to violent arguments. And despite her own infidelities and the fact that he was still engaged to Mary Dawson, when she found out that he was having another affair—with an au pair—Ruth was furious. On one occasion she drove to the house where the girl worked and, seeing her Blakely's car outside, proceeded to smash every window at the front of the house.

Then, surprisingly, for a short while, Ruth's life looked as though it might finally settle down. Blakely broke off his engagement to Mary Dawson and proposed to Ruth. She was delighted and told friends that it was a turning point in her life. The relative peace and happiness was just the eye of the storm though. Blakely was still visiting his au pair lover and quickly became tired of Ruth's possessiveness. One night in January 1955, while drunk, he punched Ruth so hard in the stomach that she miscarried his child. The years of brutal, drunken rows, dalliances with other partners, and terrible behavior finally came to a head on Easter Sunday that year.

The lover she had so much hope for had turned out no better than any of the other men in her life, so Ruth

BELOW: The gun that Ruth Ellis used to shoot David Blakely.

ABOVE: Crowds gathering outside Holloway Prison before the execution of Ruth Ellis.

made her way to the Magdala public house in Hampstead, north London. In her bag was a .38 Smith and Weston revolver given to her by Desmond Cussen who not only showed her how to use it, but also drove her to the pub that night. On seeing Blakely in the Magdala, Ruth was overwhelmed with an icy, calm fury. As she later explained to a court, "I had a peculiar idea to kill David."

When Blakely left the pub with his friend Clive Gunnell, headed towards a night of pleasure with his au pair girlfriend, he heard Ruth scream "Get out of the way Clive!" Then a bullet ripped into him and he fell. Ruth fired three more shots as Blakely lay in the gutter. His life of womanizing and drinking was over.

Ruth went on trial at the Old Bailey on June 20, 1955. The jury took just 14 minutes to find her guilty of murder, and the sentence was death by hanging. Many suggested that she had brought it upon herself, having shown no remorse in court and making it perfectly clear her one intention on the night in question was to kill her lover. Nevertheless, there was an immediate public outcry. While no-one disputed that Ruth was a murderer, the campaign against capital punishment in Britain had lately been gathering pace, and to hang a woman who had been so taken advantage of and abused by so many men was deemed too harsh. On July 13, 1955, more than 1,000 people gathered outside Holloway Prison crying for Ruth to be reprieved. They added their voices to the many petitions sent to the Home Secretary. One petition alone bore 50,000 signatures.

The protests fell on deaf ears. Ruth's head was put through a noose and moments later the trapdoor beneath fell away. Writing in the Daily Mirror newspaper that day, the popular columnist Cassandra moved the nation with the words, "If you read this after nine o'clock in the morning, the murderess Ruth Ellis will have gone. The one thing that brings stature and dignity to mankind and raises us above the beasts of the field will have been denied her—pity and the hope of ultimate redemption."

Ruth Ellis was buried in an unmarked grave within the walls of Holloway Prison. In the early 1970s the prison underwent a program of rebuilding, during which the bodies of all executed women were exhumed for reburial elsewhere. Ellis's was reburied at St. Mary's Church in Amersham, Buckinghamshire. The headstone in the churchyard was originally inscribed "Ruth Hornby 1926–1955," but in 1982 it was destroyed by her son Andy shortly before he committed suicide.

Sergeant Frederick Emmett-Dunne

Often, the victims of crimes of passion are the innocent people who happen to be close to those caught up in powerful emotions. The murder of Sergeant Reginald Watters, for example, shows how love can set an otherwise decent man to kill his best friend.

Tall, handsome Sergeant Frederick Emmett-Dunne and his five-foot, one-inch friend Sergeant Reginald Watters were stationed in Duisburg, Germany, as part of the British post-war occupation force. While in Germany, Watters met and married a beautiful ex-nightclub singer called Mia. At first, Emmett-Dunne tried to repress his feelings for his mate's wife, but the more time he spent in their company the more his passion for her grew and the more he came to resent the fact that his unremarkable, short friend had married her when she should have been his. Slowly the bonds of friendship were overwhelmed by jealousy, to the point where Emmett-Dunne was prepared to kill the man he had once shared so much with.

On November 30, 1953, the body of Reginald Watters was found hanging from the banister at his barracks on the British Army base. It was Emmett-Dunne who broke the news to Mia, telling the widow that he would be constantly at her side to help her through her ordeal. He also gave a statement to the police saying that he had driven Watters back to his quarters at 7pm the night before, bid him good night, and left. The doctor who conducted the postmortem concluded that death was caused by shock, brought on by strangulation. Watters, he wrote on his report, had committed suicide by hanging.

There was something amiss though. Despite the verdict, gossip began to circulate. It was whispered that

Watters had committed suicide because his wife was having a secret fling with his best friend. The marriage of Mia and Emmett-Dunne in England just seven months later did nothing to still the wagging tongues.

But it wasn't just gossips who were suspicious of the events. The marriage was also viewed with suspicion by one of the official army criminal investigators named Sergeant Frank Walters. He had previously been bothered by the suicide verdict, too, and did not believe that Watters was type to take his own life, no matter how serious his personal problems were. When he heard about the wedding, Walters contacted Scotland Yard to report his concerns.

In February 1955 an order arrived at British headquarters in Duisburg to exhume Watters' body. Examination by a more experienced pathologist revealed that he had died not by hanging, but by a "severe blow across the front of the throat"—just the kind of blow that might have been inflicted by someone trained in unarmed combat. At the same time

Emmett-Dunne's half-brother Ronald, who had been a private at Duisburg, confessed to his own involvement in Watters' death. He told investigators that he had helped Emmett-Dunne hang Watters up on the bannister after his panicked half-brother told him he had killed him by accident.

Emmett-Dunne was arrested at the home in Taunton, Somerset, he shared with Mia. Despite his claim that he had acted in self-defense when Watters threatened to shoot him and had only meant to stun, he was charged with murder. The case, held before a seven-man army court, was covered extensively in the British and German press. On July 1955, Emmett-Dunne was found guilty of murder and sentenced to death. However, he escaped a fate that many thought he richly deserved. West Germany had abolished capital punishment, and foreign army bases had to conform with the law of the country. Instead Emmett-Dunne was given a life sentence. He served 10 years in Britain before being released.

Dr. Yves Evenou & Simone Deschamps

Twice divorced Yves Evenou had the good fortune to find his third wife in the strikingly beautiful and young Marie-Claire. But though she was undoubtedly stunning, she could not satisfy his cravings for perverted sex games: for that he turned to an older, plain woman. And when his desire for both waned he formed a plan to get rid of them in one disgusting act.

What Simone Deschamps lacked in looks she more than made up for with her zealous participation in sexual masochism. Almost as soon as she came into his surgery one day in the mid-1950s Dr Yves Evenou realized that she was a woman with whom he could explore his secret dark lusts. Before long he had moved his sex partner into the flat below the one he shared with his wife, Marie-Claire. It was a perfect arrangement for Evenou; a loving, respectable and beautiful wife in one flat, and a subservient mistress willing to satisfy all his perverted desires, in the flat below. Evenou even told a friend, "She may not be beautiful, but she knows how to love."

A willing conspirator in the duping of Marie-Claire, Simone even made herself useful to her lover's wife, helping her with chores around the house that were too heavy for the sickly doctor's wife. But as Simone and Evenou pushed their sexual boundaries to the limit, so the doctor grew ever more tired of his wife and his lover, too, and began plotting to get rid of them both in one foul swoop. To a twisted and sadist mind such as his, the plan he hatched must have had an elegant simplicity: he would incite Simone to kill

RIGHT: Dr. Yves Evenou (center) following his lawyer, Charles Marcelpoll, in a lobby of the Palace of Justice of Paris.

Marie-Claire and then inform on her to the police. The plan also had the merit of providing one last, horribly depraved, sexual thrill.

Evenou warmed his lover up to the idea slowly. One night he told her, "My first two wives left me of their own accord but this one sticks like mustard plaster." After a day or two, he announced, "I feel that I should kill her, or maybe that you should do it for me." By the following day, after six glasses of port, the doctor appeared to make his mind up. "We must kill her," he told Simone. Without a word, she rose from her chair, went to the local hardware store, and bought a knife.

That evening Marie-Claire complained of a toothache, and her husband suggested a sleeping pill to ease the pain. As soon as she was asleep, Evenou rang the apartment below and Simone arrived within moments, naked except for a coat and shoes, which she slipped off. Then Evenou gently uncovered his wife's breast and said, "Strike here!" Simone obeyed. Marie-Claire woke in a shock as the knife plunged into her body and cried out, "Simone!" and then, "No! No!" But Evenou held her in his arms and whispered, 'There, there, everything's all right'. Befuddled with drugs and not yet feeling any pain, Marie-Claire relaxed, and Simone struck her again and again: 11 times in all. Then the lovers kissed. When it was over, Simone went to the bathroom to wash her hands, and Yves Evenou slipped out of the door. A few minutes later he arrived at the police station and told them that Simone Deschamps had murdered his wife.

What may have been an elegant plot in Evenou's mind didn't stand up to police investigations and questions. He was arrested alongside his sado-masochistic lover, but escaped trial by dying before the case could be heard. For her part in the murder, however, Simone Deschamps received a life sentence.

Dr. Renzo Ferrari

When Tranquillo Allevi drank from a bottle of liqueur that contained enough strychnine to kill 500 men, the Italian police were baffled at first, but one by one they exonerated his wife's lovers until they found the man who poisoned him.

At 38, Renata Allevi was a sophisticated woman of the world. She loved her wealthy dairy farmer husband who kept her in all the luxuries she could want, but also delighted in the intrigue and passions of her illicit liaisons and kept a stable of men to admire her. Nevertheless, the charmed life she had been leading shuddered to a halt on August 26, 1973.

Two days earlier a bottle of liqueur had arrived from Milan with a note explaining that the established Italian drinks manufacturer who made it was planning a sales campaign in the local area and asking Tranquillo Allevi if he would consider becoming the company's local representative. Allevi was an influential and highly popular man, and often received this kind of offer, so when the bottle arrived Renata thought nothing of it. She signed for it and left it on her husband's desk.

When he returned he put it in the refrigerator to cool and then forgot about it.

On the 26th, after taking his wife out to dinner at a local restaurant, Tranquillo Allevi went to his office to entertain two friends. He remembered the bottle and took it from the fridge, poured three glasses, and—while his friends politely sipped their drinks—knocked his back in one. Death came quickly. Allevi was screaming by the time the liquid hit his stomach and his body quickly went into uncontrollable spasms. He was rushed to hospital but died soon after he was admitted. The diagnosis was obvious, for his friends too showed signs of poisoning, though mercifully their small sips saved them from death.

The police immediately suspected Renata, but it was apparent that her grief was genuine, and she made no

ABOVE: Renzo Ferrari gesturing in front of microphones as he answers questions by the president of a Court of Assizes in Imperia on the Italian Riviera, during his 1964 trial.

secret of the fact that she had signed for the bottle and even suggested to her husband that he put it in the fridge. Perplexed they looked elsewhere, but Allevi was a popular man and had no enemies that anyone knew of. Then, reluctantly, Renata admitted that she had three lovers with whom she regularly met: her husband's book-keeper, an army officer, and the veterinary surgeon who looked after Allevi's herds.

Another clue was the bottle itself, which had been sent from Milan on August 23. Checks with the drinks company confirmed that though over 100 complimentary bottles had been sent out, Allevi's name was not on the mailing list and the accompanying letter was not on the company's headed paper. Tests showed that a massive dose of strychnine had been injected into the bottle through the cork.

The police began to question Renata's lovers. The first two had alibis to prove that they had been nowhere near Milan the day the parcel was posted. The book-keeper had been with a client in San Remo, while the army officer had been in Tuscany on maneuvers. Detectives were left with the veterinary surgeon, Dr. Renzo Ferrari, who had been in Milan on that very day to renew his professional license. He had also purchased strychnine. And a check on the town hall offices Ferrari used in his post as a local government officer, revealed the typewriter upon which the accompanying letter had been written.

On September 1, 1973, Ferrari was charged with the murder of Tranquillo Allevi. At his trial the truth finally emerged. He pleaded not guilty, and his defense counsel told the court that he had no motive. Ferrari, they argued, had recently become engaged to the daughter of a wealthy family and had broken off his purely sexual relationship with Renata. He was looking forward to a good future and there was no reason to jeopardize it. Renata, however, painted a very different picture for the jury and one that fit the facts. On the witness stand she said that her husband had found out about the affair and that while she saw other men for pleasure it was him she loved, so she had agreed to finish with Ferrari. On being notified that their affair was over, Ferrari refused to accept it and when she told him, "I will never return to you", he had replied, "We will see about that."

A representative of the drinks company supplied the final, damning, piece of evidence. He stated under oath that no sample had been sent to Mr Allevi. However, one bottle had been dispatched, with an invitation on company notepaper, to one Dr. Renzo Ferrari.

The jury did not need any further evidence. Ferrari was found guilty of murder with premeditation on May 15, 1974. His combined sentence amounted to 30 years, including consecutive terms for the attempted murder of Allevi's two drinking companions. Although he has never admitted to it, it is very possible that the murderer had hoped that Allevi and his wife would open the bottle together and that he would thus have killed both of them. Once the bottle was delivered, Ferrari had no way of controlling who drank the poisoned liqueur, which suggests that he did not care which of the Allevis he murdered.

Sheila Garvie and Brian Tevendale

In retrospect it is hardly surprising that Max Garvie was eventually murdered, for the sex games he delighted in grew so astonishingly depraved that it was almost inevitable that sooner or later there would be an emotional backlash.

In 1955, **Sheila Watson** considered herself lucky to have landed Max Garvie for a husband. He was handsome, rich, and the owner of a large farm in Fordoun, Kincardineshire, Scotland. Over the following years the couple had two daughters and a son and had Max not been so bored of his tranquil existence the family might have enjoyed a happy family life. At first Garvie tried to liven up his life with the expensive toys of the rich. He filled his driveway with fast cars and bought a private plane, but nothing seemed to bring the satisfaction he craved and he eventually began looking for excitement elsewhere.

It started innocently. Garvie created his own so-called "nudist colony," and groups of his wealthy, thrill-seeking friends were invited to weekend parties where they would frolic naked within a triangle of trees and thick bushes Garvie had planted for just that reason. It was not long, however, before the guests' inhibitions were set aside completely and Garvie's nude parties turned into sex orgies.

Sheila Garvie wasn't interested, and tried to ignore the naked flesh and debauched scenes in her garden. Instead, she tried to shield the children from what was happening outside the house and shrugged off her husband's continual demands that she join in the fun. Eventually, however, she was worn down by his pestering. Sheila gave in and went on to become a willing, and even enthusiastic, member of the group.

By this time West Cairnbeg Farm had become known locally as "Kinky Cottage," and guests at the house were playing a dangerous game of jealousy and broken rules. Garvie took his sexual adventures further with homosexual couplings and then brought 20-year-old Brian Tevendale into his home—not for his own

pleasure but for Sheila's. His wife was appalled at the idea. She saw sex sessions in the company of her husband as acceptable, but not the intimacy of one-to-one lovemaking.

Nevertheless, she gave in again. One night in 1967, when Tevendale was staying over, his bedroom door was suddenly opened and a naked, shivering Sheila shoved into the room by her husband. Garvie had at last broken his wife's will. Now the games took a new turn with Garvie and Tevendale tossing a coin to see who would sleep with Sheila. When Garvie lost he insisted the three go to bed together. Then Garvie started an affair with Tevendale's sister, Trudi Birse, wife of a policeman. Trudi joined in four-in-a-bed romps with the Garvies and her own brother. Trudi's husband even

ABOVE: Sheila Garvie on her way to the High Court at Stonehaven, Scotland, in 1968.

joined in, though Max thoughtfully arranged another female partner for him.

Still Garvie craved new sensual pleasures and further erotic adventures. Growing bored with Trudi, he suggested to Sheila that they both move on to new bedmates. Sheila refused. The one thing her husband had not considered was that amid all the debauched coupling real affection might blossom, but now his wife was passionately in love with Brian Tevendale. Used to getting his own way, Garvie tried to come between them. The man who had forced them together now tried to prize them apart.

On the morning of May 15, 1968, Sheila Garvie reported her husband missing to the police. She said when she had woken up that morning, Garvie was not in bed or anywhere to be found. Whether to cover her tracks or because she was genuinely innocent, Sheila confided in her mother, Edith Watson, that she thought Tevendale had killed her husband, and an appalled Mrs Watson went straight to the police.

Max Garvie's putrefying remains were eventually found in the drains of Laurieston Castle, St. Cyrus—Tevendale's home village—on August 17, 1968. The police's investigations led them straight to the depraved goings-on at the farm and Sheila Garvie, Brian Tevendale, and one of his friends, Alan Peters, were arrested and charged with Garvie's murder.

The sensational trial began at Aberdeen High Court on November 19, 1968. While details of the sordid events became public, Sheila and Tevendale accused each other of the murder. Sheila claimed she woke in the middle of the night to discover Tevendale and Peters had murdered her husband; Tevendale said the killing was Sheila's idea and he had gone along with it because of his infatuation with her. The prosecution, however, maintained that Sheila and Tevendale had plotted the murder together in order to stop Garvie from splitting them up. They suggested that on the night Garvie died, Sheila had slipped out of the marital bed to let Tevendale and Peters into the house and given them a gun. She then watched as Tevendale used it to smash Max's skull before putting a pillow over his face and shooting him in the head. The men then wrapped the body in a blanket, put it in the boot of Peters's car, and dumped it in the drains of Laurieston Castle. Throughout the proceedings, both the jury and the nation were horrified by the perverse events and the crime itself. One juror fainted when the yellowed skull of Max Garvie was produced as part of the prosecution evidence.

In the end, the prosecution prevailed—barely. The jury unanimously found Tevendale guilty of murder and Sheila was also found guilty by a majority verdict—enough under Scottish law to sentence her. The case against Peters was not proven.

Tevendale and Sheila were both released from prison in 1978, but never saw each other again choosing to lead anonymous lives. Tevendale married and became the landlord of a public house in Perthshire. He died in 2003. Sheila married twice—she was divorced once and then widowed—and led a quiet life running a bed and breakfast.

William Gardiner

The so-called Peasenhall Mystery of 1902, is one of the most notable of murder cases in British criminal history with a cast of characters reads like an Agatha Christie novel. William Gardiner was a Sunday school teacher, devout church minister, and married father of six; the victim—Gardiner's pregnant lover—a choir girl at the village church. Officially "unsolved" it is likely that Gardiner would have been convicted had it not been for the alibi provided by the very wife he had been cheating on.

The affair between 23-year-old Rose Harsent and Gardiner was much gossiped about in the small Suffolk village of Peasenhall. She was a domestic servant who sang in the choir and he taught Sunday school and delivered sermons from the pulpit. While it was rumored that Gardiner was only one of several men that Rose was involved with, the pair appear to have been irresistibly attracted to one another. Some said that the vicar had been called upon to intervene after they were caught in a compromising situation, but even his warnings had failed to cool their passion and the secret trysts continued.

On June 1, 1902, Rose was found dead by her father at Providence House where she worked. Her half-naked body was at the foot of the stairs with the throat cut from ear to ear. There were wounds on her shoulders and her nightdress was burned. It seemed that whoever had killed Rose had tried to set fire to her to destroy the evidence. Further examinations of her body revealed that she had been pregnant.

It did not take long for Gardiner to become the prime suspect. A police search of Rose's room soon turned up a note in his handwriting addressed to her and arranging a secret midnight meeting. He was arrested two days later.

Gardiner's trial began on November 7, and the case against him was strong: A bloodied knife had been found at his home (though Gardiner said he had used it to kill rabbits) and neighbors spoke of a late-night bonfire in the Gardiner's garden on May 31. The police suggested that Gardiner and his wife had been burning his blood-stained clothes. Nevertheless, Mrs Gardiner insisted that they had passed an unremarkable evening together before retiring to bed where they had both stayed until morning.

Of the 12 jurors, 11 thought Gardiner guilty, but without a unanimous verdict a retrial was ordered to begin on January 21, 1903. Again, the jury failed to reach a unanimous decision, this time with 10 of their number finding him innocent. Arrangements were quickly made for yet another trial, but before it began the Home Office decided that there was no prospect of securing a conviction and lodged a verdict of *nolle prosequi*—not proven. The case against Gardiner was dismissed and he was released from custody, having neither been convicted or acquitted.

Lilian Getkate

Every so often, someone slips through loopholes in the law, and so it proved in the case of Lilian Getkate. A former Brownie leader and church-goer, Lilian fully expected to serve a prison sentence for the crime of shooting her husband with his own rifle, but despite failing to convince many that she had good cause to kill, the jury found her guilty of the lesser charge of manslaughter and sentenced her to just 200 hours of community service. In a second stroke of luck, Lilian's conviction preceded a change in the law by just three weeks. Under the new ruling anyone convicted of manslaughter using a firearm was to be sentenced to at least four years jail time.

Lilian's was a problematic case. Her defense lawyer told the jury that she had been subjected to years of constant abuse by her husband, Maury. During their 16 years of marriage she had been dragged by her hair, made a virtual prisoner in her own home, raped, and threatened with death. Lilian also claimed that what finally provoked her to kill was her husband threatening to sexually abuse their daughter. According to a report in the Canadian newspaper, the Ottawa Citizen, Maury Getkate had been a tall, well-built man; a "paramilitary buff and aspiring ninja" who had a collection of "exotic weaponry." Two psychiatrists who examined and interviewed Lilian testified that she fitted the criteria for "battered woman syndrome."

The evidence was not so clear-cut though. Relatives and friends of the couple gave a different story, saying that to all outward appearances the Gatkates had been a happy, ordinary couple, devoted to their children and Lilian more than satisfied to be a stay-at-home mother. Maury Getkate, they said, was a hard-working, successful professional admired by his colleagues.

In fact, as crown prosecutor Julianne Parfett pointed out to the court, the only evidence they had for Lilian's plight came from Lilian herself. "No one could corroborate it," Parfett stated. "Not a bruise, not a hospital record, not a police report. Nothing... that's what is most troubling about this one. We simply say, 'Yes, you were abused. Fine. You walk.' That's what this sentence was all about. I think it's an appalling message to send to the public." With no third-person testimony or physical evidence to corroborate Lilian's tales, Parfett suggested that, at most, she may have suffered "moderate abuse."

Nevertheless, a jury made up of 10 women and two men found Lilian guilty only of the lesser charge of manslaughter, and she was ordered to do community service and attend meetings of Co-Dependents Anonymous, a support group for emotionally dependent people. It was not a verdict that pleased Ms Parfett. After hearing the sentence, she said, "The decision to spare her jail sends a message that women can kill, claim they have been abused, fail to prove it, and remain free." Lilian's defense lawyer, Patrick McCann, was quick to respond, saying, "There's a long tradition in Canada that women who have been abused by their husbands or partners and have reacted to that and killed the man, have been convicted of manslaughter and not received custodial sentences. This is nothing new."

In the middle of the legal fuss was Lilian Getkate. She was as surprised as anyone to be walking free. And her surprise must have turned to relief when it was announced that from January 1996 there would be mandatory prison sentences of at least four years for manslaughter offences in which firearms are used. Lilian shot her husband in December 1995.

Chester Gillette

Born to a deeply religious family, Chester Gillette traveled around the United States during his formative years. By the time he reached age 22 in 1905, Gillette had settled in New York City where he worked as a foreman at his wealthy uncle's shirt factory. It was here that he met the pretty young secretary Grace Brown, who was just 18 years old.

Grace fell for the dashing nephew of the boss, and in a whirl of passion she was soon sleeping with him. The result was a pregnancy. Expecting Gillette to make an honest woman of her, Grace returned to her family home to come to terms with approaching motherhood and to await a marriage proposal. It never came. Instead, Grace discovered that Gillette had never been faithful and was now openly seeing other women. The final blow came when she discovered that the man she loved had met an attractive and wealthy socialite at a dance, and that he had become engaged to her. Her heartbroken letters to her lover became increasingly desperate, but still Gillette would not acknowledge her or the coming baby. Eventually, with nowhere left to turn, Grace threatened to tell Gillette's uncle the whole story and expose his dreadful conduct.

The threat seemed to work. In July 1906, Gillette told Grace to pack for a weekend trip away. Excited, and possibly believing that the trip would involve a wedding ceremony, she packed her entire wardrobe. Gillette, meanwhile, packed almost nothing.

At first the couple checked into a rented cottage on Tupper Lake in Herkimer County, but the resort was too busy for what Gillette had in mind. At his insistence, they moved onto Big Moose Lake, taking separate rooms in a hotel there. Gillette then hired a rowing boat under the name of Carl Graham (careful to matching the initials on his suitcase) and rowed his pregnant teenage lover out onto the water. When they were some distance way from the shore, Gillette battered Grace with a tennis racket, then tipped her over the side, and rowed back alone. The unconscious Grace was left to drown. Gillette's social climbing ambitions were safe.

Back on shore, Gillette tried to cover his tracks by moving on to the Arrowhead Hotel on Eagle Bay. However, he made a fatal error in asking the check-in clerk if there had been any reported drownings. When

ABOVE: Chester Gillette's heartless murder of his one-time lover led to his eventual execution.

ABOVE: Grace Brown's only crime was to fall in love with the wrong man—who turned out to be a killer.

Grace Brown's body surfaced the next day, the clerk remembered Gillette's strange question, and the killer came under immediate suspicion. The tennis racket used to bludgeon Grace was found on the shore of Big Moose Lake, and under police questioning Gillette was nervous and shifty.

In court, the jury heard the extent of Gillette's callousness as Grace's heart-rending letters to her lover were read out, one by one, by the lawyers acting for the prosecution. He was found guilty of murder on December 4, 1906, and sentenced to death in the electric chair.

Gary Grinhaff

While some killers' fury vents itself in an uncontrollable outburst of deadly rage, others channel it into a cold, calm plan for revenge. Convinced that the affair that his wife had confessed to was still continuing, Gary Grinhaff approached murder—and his own suicide—in a highly methodical manner.

Grinhaff discovered the affair his wife, Tracey, had been having in February 2008. A few weeks later he confronted her, and in order to try and resolve the situation peacefully her lover and his wife were called over to discuss it. It was an unusual step, but seemed to work; the unfaithful pair agreed that they would end their illicit relationship.

Over the following weeks though, Grinhaff became convinced that Tracey had not kept her promise so, ignoring his wife's protests of innocence, he set about to prove that she was still arranging secret love trysts. First he bugged her car so that he could listen to conversations and fitted it with a tracking device. Then he secretly bought another car in which he could follow her undetected. By May 1, he had the proof he needed. Tracey was a cheat, and with the same efficient calm Grinhaff made plans for retribution.

At 6am on the morning of May 3, 2008, the Grinhaff's three-year-old daughter Niamh woke her older sister Chloe. She was standing on the landing outside her parents' bedroom crying because she couldn't find her mother. Thirteen-year-old Chloe went to investigate and found her mother and father's bed empty and the duvet laying on the floor. Downstairs she found the note in the kitchen pinned to the cooker hood. It was in her father's handwriting and gave her certain instructions. The teenager phoned a neighbor who told the girls not to go to school and contacted the police.

When the police arrived they found signs of an attack in the Grinhaff's bedroom, though an effort had obviously been made to make it tidy and to hide bloodstains from the two girls. Later, the bodies were discovered. Tracey Grinhaff's was found in the shed at the back of her garden. She had been strangled and bludgeoned to death with a heavy object. Shortly after, police found Gary Grinhaff's corpse in woodland nearby. He had killed himself by cutting into his own leg and arm with the saw attachment to his cordless electric drill. They later also found the car that Grinhaff had used to follow his wife, with notes inside so that his daughters wouldn't discover them. One was addressed to the wife of Tracey's lover and read, "This cannot go on; this is my only way out."

At the inquest assistant deputy coroner Donald Coutts-Wood said that Grinhaff had gone to considerable lengths to confirm his wife had resumed her affair and once satisfied had set out to kill her. He recorded verdicts that Mrs Grinhaff was unlawfully killed and that her husband committed suicide.

Albert Guay

There are no words to describe the sheer depravity of Albert Guay's crime. Even if we cannot understand the minds of many of the murderers who have been pressed to kill by their passion we can, at least, begin to imagine how a person may have come to feel so violently angry that they wished to punish the person who caused their pain or stood in the way of their future happiness. But Guay's crime goes far beyond that, for in planning to murder the wife who stood between him and his teenage mistress he saw no obstacle in causing the deaths of 22 other people, four of them children.

Joseph-Albert Guay was born on January 12, 1919. The youngest of five children he was spoiled as a youngster and the temper tantrums that followed his not getting exactly what he wanted were something that he would take into adulthood with him. As a young man Guay sold watches and jewelry on commission and when World War II broke out, he got a job at Canadian Arsenals Limited at St. Malo. There he met the woman who was to become his wife, Rita Morel. When the arsenal closed in 1945, Guay left with a little money, which he spent on buying a jewelry and watch repair shop. Life should have been sweet for the shop owner and his new wife, but from the start the couple argued frequently, and the fights grew worse after the birth of their child. The shop was not doing well and the financial strain was added to by a new tension in the house. Like many immature men, Guay felt slighted that he was no longer the center of attention in his own household. His natural inclination toward jealousy and possessiveness grew more pronounced as he realized his needs now came second to that of his son. Eventually, after eight years of marriage, he decided that the only way he would feel important again was to find someone who doted on him as his wife once did.

The girl he chose was 17-year-old nightclub waitress Marie-Ange Robitaille, who liked to be called Mary Angel. To help prevent his wife finding out about his pursuit of a teenager, Guay gave a false name when he first met her and it became the name he used throughout their relationship, which—despite his own family's financial worries—was conducted at an apartment Guay paid for. He also promised to marry her. Duped by his lies, Marie-Ange had no reason to doubt that she was not being seriously courted by a gentleman called Roger Angers who dearly wished to walk down the aisle with her.

But despite his careful tactics to avoid discovery Rita found out everything, and chose the place to confront her husband to cause the maximum damage to his affair. When Guay visited Mary-Ange at her parents' home one day, he found his wife waiting for him and the

RIGHT: Albert Guay, pictured with his wife Rita, who was one of the victims of the plane crash that he callously engineered.

secret life he had built completely destroyed. Mary-Ange was ordered out of the house by her appalled mother and father and the Guays soon followed, arguing viciously. When they returned home Rita packed some clothes and took the couple's five-year-old daughter to live at her mother's house.

If Rita had meant to finish his relationship, she failed. None of this seemed to bother Guay. He continued to see his young lover, and in most respects his life was little changed. The confrontation had, however, altered the relationship with Mary-Ange forver. Now she insisted that Guay make an honest woman of her and told him that if he didn't then she would end the affair. With divorce in the largely Catholic province of Quebec rare in the 1940s, Guay realized that the only way could marry his pretty young lover was to bring about 28-year-old Rita's death.

Initially, Guay considered killing his wife with poison, but he was afraid of discovery. After all, there were numerous people who knew he had a good motive for killing his wife. Instead, he concocted a twisted plan that he thought no-one would ever suspect. He traveled frequently by plane in his business as a jeweler to deliver or pick up items for his shop and came to the conclusion that if he could get his wife to take his place while he planted a bomb that would bring the plane down then there was every chance of the crime remaining undiscovered. And if he could time the bomb so the wreckage landed in the St. Lawrence River, any evidence would be washed away.

The more he examined his idea, the more he liked it, but there was a drawback. For a murder on this scale he would need the help of others. Unfortunately, he knew just where to find them.

The rewards that Guay must have promised those willing to join his evil scheme must have been huge, but he soon had his co-conspirators. The first was one of his employees, wheelchair-bound watchmaker Genereux Ruest, who would help him build and package a time bomb. Although Ruest had worked in the munitions factory alongside Guay, he did not have the detailed knowledge required for bomb-making or, indeed, how to go about blowing up a plane so he and Guay decided that a trial run would be needed. In preparation, the pair consulted local explosives experts, using the bizarre cover story that they needed to dynamite a pond. With all the information he needed and with help from Guay, Ruest worked on the bomb-making project from his wheelchair. He eventually created a simple, but effective, timed device from 20 sticks of dynamite, an alarm clock, and a battery. The second person that Guay enlisted was 41-year-old Margeuritte Pitre. She was Ruest's married sister and another former mistress. It would be her job to deliver the bomb to its destination.

All Guay had to do now was persuade Rita to make the plane journey. Guay insisted to his estranged wife that though their marriage was all but over, there was no reason why she shouldn't continue to help him with the business. It was imperative, he told her, that she should go to Baie Corneau to collect some jewels he had ordered from the mining community. Rita refused, but her estranged husband insisted that he was too busy to go himself and pointed out that her income depended on him doing well. When she protested again he told her that he had already bought the ticket. He failed to mention that he had also taken out a $10,000 insurance policy on her life, on top of another for $5,000 that he had purchased back in 1942. Finally, Rita agreed, though the couple argued fiercely as Guay drove her to Quebec City airport on the morning of September 9, 1949. They continued their row inside.

Meanwhile, Pitre was also on her way to the airport in a taxi. She had with her a very heavy parcel, which she told airport authorities was a religious statuette that had to be delivered to a Mr Larouche at an address in Baie Comeau. The 26 pound parcel was duly checked in as freight.

Shortly afterward, Rita boarded the Canadian Pacific Airlines DC-3 together with 22 other passengers. The plane was five minutes late leaving Quebec City and took off at 10.25am, a delay that upset Quay's carefully laid plan. It climbed into the sky and headed northeast toward the St. Lawrence River. And exploded 20 minutes later, scattering debris over the shore of the river rather than into the water. A fisherman near Sault-au-Cochon, 50 miles north of Quebec City, later told how he saw the smoking plane crash toward Cap Tormente on the wooded north shore of the river. Other witnesses said the plane's engines were still running as it hit the ground, which meant that investigators could immediately rule out engine failure as the cause of the crash.

Five workers at a nearby railway line witnessed the terrifying sight, too, and rushed to the scene. But there was nothing they could do. As flames flashed through the aircraft it was clear there would be no survivors. One of the rail workers gave a report to Montreal's La Patrie newspaper, saying: "Arms, legs, and severed heads were lying on the ground. The forward part of the plane looked intact. The bodies were piled up in there as if they had been thrown forward when the plane crashed... There was nothing we could do so we rushed to alert the railway authorities."

News of the disaster was soon being broadcast on radio stations throughout the province and police and Mounties descended on the crash site. The dead included the four crew, four children, and three American executives from the Kennecott Copper Corporation. Guay and his co-conspirators had succeeded in the murder of Rita Guay, but, in total, the lives of 22 other people were also lost. And all so that Albert Guay could marry his teenage sweetheart.

However, Guay would never make his trip down the aisle. Forensic analysis of the plane's debris soon revealed traces of dynamite and investigators concluded the plane had crashed following the explosion of a time bomb in the forward baggage compartment. Within days, Pitre, Guay, and Ruest were arrested. The investigation into the explosion had thrown up many clues, but the one that led straight to Guay was found in a simple tally of the freight list. All but one of the items on board were from regular shippers, and were easily checked. There was, however, no record of the sender of the "religious statuette." Nevertheless, a conversation with the taxi driver who took Pitre to the airport revealed her address and he also remembered that the lady dressed in black had specifically warned him not to drive over any bumps in the road. The driver recalled the woman had added, "These aren't eggs I'm carrying."

When police called at the home of Margueritte Pitre she wasn't there. In fact, she was in hospital recovering from a failed suicide she had attempted after realizing the enormity of the crime she had helped commit.

Believing that the police were already watching her, Margueritte had taken an overdose of sleeping tablets. She lived, but only to face death by less gentle means. Under interrogation she maintained that she had not known what the package she had delivered contained, but no-one believed her. Neither did anyone believe her story that Guay had threatened to bankrupt her if she didn't help him, though the tale that he had encouraged her to commit suicide after the crash seemed slightly more plausible.

Before his arrest Guay had presented himself to the world as a man deeply in mourning for his beloved wife. He urged investigators to "get to the bottom of this" and carried a large cross of flowers to Rita's funeral and placed it on her coffin, telling a priest, "If God wanted it, I accept." He was, however, swiftly forced to drop the pretence after he was arrested on September 23, 1949. and charged with murder.

Reust's arrest followed soon after. The three killers appeared at separate trials at the Supreme Court of Canada throughout 1950 and early 1951. Guay was charged with the killing of 22 people along with the assassination of his wife and found guilty. Imposing the death sentence, the judge told him, "Your crime is infamous. It has no name."

Albert Guay was hanged on January 19, 1951, in the Bordeaux Jail near Montreal. As was the ritual there, a chime sounded seven times to announce the execution of a man. (It sounded ten times to announce a woman's death.) Newspapers reported that his last words were, "Well, at least I die famous."

Reust fruitlessly claimed that he had not known his homemade bomb would be used to kill people. There were witnesses, however, who had seen him on the terrace of a hotel on the day of the crash; a vantage point he had chosen because it offered a fine view of the aircraft's course and, therefore, of the crash itself. Ruest was taken to the gallows in his wheelchair and hanged on July 25, 1952.

Pitre's trial began in March 1951, too late for Guay to testify against her as he had done against Reust in an effort to avoid the death penalty. Although she protested her innocence throughout, she was also found guilty and became the last women to be executed in Canada on January 9, 1953.

Catherine Hayes

The death of the last woman ever to be executed at Tyburn, London's infamous killing ground, was as gory as the one she inflicted on her husband. Catherine Hayes had an appetite for the wild side of life. She enjoyed nothing more than heavy drinking and romping with her two teenage lovers. However, her fun was spoiled by the presence of a husband. For Catherine the answer was simple: John Hayes must die.

The method Hayes chose for murder was direct and extreme, as might be expected of a woman who delighted in her own wildness. And it didn't take much to convince her two strong and virile young lovers to help. Catherine Hayes, Thomas Billings, and Thomas Wood prepared for their evening's work by drinking at the Brawn's Head tavern in London's New Bond Street. They then returned to the Hayes' home and, pretending to be friendly, plied John Hayes with enormous amounts of drink.

After drinking six pints of wine, Hayes staggered to his bed and collapsed. Even had he been conscious Hayes would have been in no state to defend himself from what happened next. Billings smashed him on the back of the head with a coal hatchet, fracturing his skull, and as Hayes gurgled in his death throes, Wood entered the room and hit him twice more. Then Catherine joined her young bedmates, and all three of them decapitated the body.

Hayes' head was taken in a blood filled bucket to be thrown in the River Thames, while the rest of his body was dismembered and stuffed in a trunk that was hidden in the local woods. However, in their haste and drunkenness, Wood and Billings made a mistake. Hayes' head was not washed away on the tide, but came to rest on the river's shore. Night watchmen soon discovered it, and the next day it was paraded on a pole around the streets of London in a ghastly identity parade.

LEFT: Catherine Hayes hacking off the head of her husband John Hayes with the aid of her young lovers, Thomas Billings and Thomas Wood.

RIGHT: Catherine Hayes being strangled and burned at the stake for the murder of her husband. The flames were so high that the executioner dropped the rope, and she was in fact burned to death.

It did not take the law long to catch up the murderous trio, and all three were found guilty at the Old Bailey, London's central criminal court, on April 30, 1726. Catherine Hayes and her lovers each received a death sentence. While in Newgate Prison awaiting her execution, Catherine sent letters to Wood and Billings showing remorse for involving them in the horrendous act. In a perverse twist, it was later whispered that she had also confessed that Billings was actually her son from a previous affair. Wood caught a fever in prison and died before he could be executed.

On May 14, Catherine Hayes was driven on a cart to be burned at the stake. Reports of the time tell us that, "She was fasten'd to the stake by an iron collar round her neck, and an iron chain round her body, having an halter also about her neck, which the Executioner pulled when she began to shriek. In about an hour's time she was reduced to ashes."

Frances Howard & Robert Carr

For the young Frances Howard, daughter of the Earl of Suffolk, the temptations of sexual adventures at the court of King James I proved too great to resist. Caught up in a web of passion that may have involved the king himself, she conspired to poison her lover's other sexual partner.

Young, beautiful, and from an old noble family, Frances Howard was an excellent marriage prospect. She was duly married off to the teenage Earl of Essex in 1610. However, either his sexual interests lay elsewhere or he was simply too young to appreciate the pleasures of the bed chamber. The marriage was not consummated, and soon after Frances' new husband left court bound for a long stay in France.

The passionate young woman, left alone in a court simmering with sexual intrigue, soon found herself tempted to join in and before long was sharing her bed with a young, handsome page called Robert Carr. While Carr was also involved in a homosexual relationship with Thomas Overbury, who was 11 years Carr's senior, he seems to have been more than happy to satisfy Frances' appetites. In addition to this pair of sexual partners, it was also whispered that Carr was the king's bedmate too! He was certainly much favored by the monarch, and while Carr and Frances pleasured each other on nights that Carr didn't spend in someone else's bed, he rose quickly in the king's service. Having been given a position in the Royal court, Carr, in turn, employed Overbury as his secretary.

Trouble began to brew with the return the Earl of Essex, Frances' husband. The earl was now eager to prove himself a man and whisked his wife off to the country in order to finally consummate their marriage. Sadly for him, his clumsy approaches were rejected by a woman who was, by now, more used to the expert touch of her youbg bisexual lover. Frances refused to have sex with him, and the frustrated earl instead sought a divorce. The marriage was dissolved by the Archbishop of Canterbury.

The divorce came as a shock to Thomas Overbury. Convinced that a now single Frances would steal Carr away from him , he became hysterical and made such a public scene that King James had him thrown into the cells at the Tower of London. In fact, both Frances and Carr were eager to be rid of Overbury, whose revelations were an embarrassment to both of them. With the help of Sir Gervase Elwes, Governor of the Tower, and a chemist's assistant, they conspired to have the poison mercuric sublimate administered to Overbury in his cell. It was a foolhardy plot, for while Overbury might be imprisoned for the moment in order to stop his tongue, he was known to be one of the king's homosexual lovers. The king would be furious if the poisoning were discovered. Nevertheless, the plot went ahead. Overbury died on September 15, 1613, after enduring five months of agony.

It looked as though the murder would go undetected, but—in another unexpected twist—the chemist's assistant was struck down with a fatal illness and made a deathbed confession. Elwes and three other men involved in the plot were put on trial and executed in late 1615, while Carr and Howard were tried the following year and also sentenced to death. However, possibly due to the king's lingering affection for Carr, the penalty was waived, and the pair were instead confined in the Tower. After six years of imprisonment, they were allowed to return to their homes in the country. After all that had happened, their passion had turned to mutual hatred. Howard died of a disease of the womb when she was 39; Carr lived on. It is said that a while later, King James held his former lover and sobbed uncontrollably on his shoulder.

Gus Huberman

What must be one of the strangest cases in the history of crime began as a simple extramarital affair and ended with a husband shot dead. In between, Gus Huberman's older mistress literally treated him like a pet. Imprisoned in the attic, he was fed, watered, and played with as the mood took her.

Gus Huberman attracted Dotty Walburger's attention when he was just 16 years old. While her husband Bert was wealthy and successful, he was much given to the pleasures of the table and had grown so obese that he could no longer climb the stairs. For a woman who had her own appetites, which had nothing to do with food, the young and energetic boy who worked for a local paint company was a stark contrast to the man she had married. It was not long before the teenager and Dotty were conducting a passionate affair,

Noticing the difference in his wife and suspicious of the relationship with her new young friend, Bert Walburger hired a private detective to trail them and it didn't take long for the truth to be revealed. Faced with proof, Dotty confessed her infidelity and asked for a divorce, but Walburger refused, fearing that the court would award Dotty—and thus her lover—with a large portion of his fortune.

Unable to get rid of her husband and forced to promise that she would give her young lover up, Dotty took desperate measures. She knew that Bert was in no condition to reach the top parts of the house and her solution, while bizarre, was elegantly simple: she smuggled Huberman into the attic. Now she could indulge herself whenever she pleased while never appearing to leave the house. Whenever the Walburgers' moved home—which they did often as Bert's business flourished—Huberman secretly came with them. Dotty was careful to always insist on a tall house with a large attic space.

The situation might have continued indefinitely, but for a violent argument that broke out between Bert Walburger and his wife on August 29, 1922. Hearing it from the attic and fearing for his mistress's safety, Huberman crept down the stairs carrying a revolver that he would later tell a court he always kept handy in case of burglars. He arrived just in time to see Dotty punched to the floor. As his wife fell, Walburger looked up to find himself being watched by his wife's lover, who he had believed to have been long gone. In a fresh rage, Walburger attacked Huberman and during the fight the gun went off. Walburger lay dead. Dotty later claimed the whole incident had happened while she hid in a wardrobe.

Gus Huberman's trial lasted five weeks, during which the press began calling him "The Phantom in the Attic." While the details of the case were undeniably shocking, Huberman's plight roused enormous sympathy. He was just a young boy who had been seduced and then kept like an animal by a woman more than old enough to know better. Finally though, it was a moving speech by Huberman's lawyer that saved him from the charge of murder. Earl Wakeman, defending the lad, told the court that his client was an orphan who had known misery all his life.

Huberman was found guilty, but not of murder but the lesser charge of manslaughter and sentenced to three years in prison. However, he had served longer than this while awaiting trial and was allowed to go free at once. By the time Dotty Walburger was put on trial separately, Huberman had found himself a wife. Dotty was also acquitted when the legal system felt Huberman had been through enough and did not deserve to appear at a court again.

Lila Jimerson and Nancy Bowen

When artist Henri Marchand had a casual fling with Native-American Lila Jimerson, he said it was of no great consequence to him; just another brief sexual encounter in a long line. It was a fling that would end in murder, however. But though the woman who actually committed the deed was easy to find, the case proved so difficult to untangle that we will probably never know who really plotted to kill Clothilde Marchand. Nevertheless, it is interesting to note that before the jury reached their final verdict, Marchand had taken a new, young wife.

On March 6, 1930, Nancy Bowen, a 66-year-old Cayuga Indian from the nearby Cattaraugus Reservation walked into the home of Henri Marchand, artist for Buffalo's Natural History Museum. Inside the house, Bowen confronted Marchand's wife Clothilde and asked her, "Are you a witch?" Taken aback by the question, Mrs Marchand jokingly replied yes. On hearing the answer, Bowen beat Clothilde with a hammer, stuffed chloroform-soaked paper down her throat, and left her for dead.

When the Marchands' youngest son Henri came home from school he found his mother sprawled across the first floor landing and ran to the nearby museum, bringing home his father and two brothers. At first it was thought that Clothilde had died from falling down the stairs, but the medical examiner soon found bloody gashes, the odor of chloroform, and signs of a furious struggle on the body of the tiny Frenchwoman. The police were brought in and after questioning Henri Marchand and an associate who boarded with him, began looking for 39-year-old Lila "Red Lilac" Jimerson.

She was arrested alongside Bowen, who had retained broken pieces from Clothilde's glasses and scraps of her bloodstained clothing. But what appeared a straightforward murder for revenge would prove anything but. The court would have to sift through strange accusations, denials, and counter accusations to try and make some sense of the case. Throughout the trial there was also a strong smell of racism, with District Attorney Guy Moore at one point referring to Jimerson as a "filthy Indian."

The prosecution alleged that Lila Jimerson—determined to exact revenge for her callous treatment at Marchand's hands—had fixed upon Clothilde's reputation as a white witch as a means of getting back at him. The French woman, like many of her nation, enjoyed picking and eating wild mushrooms and her love of these "strange hellish vegetables" was considered evidence among some of the Native-American community that she practiced magic. So Jimerson convinced Nancy Bowen, whose husband Charley had recently died, that Clothilde had used her dark powers to cause his death. Bowen was thus primed to exact Jimerson's revenge for her by killing her faithless lover's wife.

During the first trial, Marchand admitted the affair, but told the court it had come about as a matter of professional necessity between artist and model. He added that he had had more affairs than he could remember, dismissing Jimerson as a minor fling. The rest of the trail did not proceed well. Jimerson, who suffered from tuberculosis, collapsed. The federal government also attempted to meddle with the proceedings by enlisting the help of a top-flight lawyer, Richard Harkness Templeton, to defend Jimerson, leaving District Attorney Moore incensed and shouting in court for Templeton to be removed. At the end of the turbulent hearing no verdict was reached.

By the time a second trial came to court, 53-year-old Marchand was remarried to an 18-year old girl and, with the financial support of the Seneca and Cayuga tribes, Jimerson had hired an excellent attorney. Jimerson continued to deny the charge and accused Marchand of the killing, saying that he had told her he wanted to hire assassins to kill his wife. Then in a dramatic reversal—and from a hospital bed—she changed her plea to guilty for second degree murder. Soon she retracted that plea, then admitted first degree murder, then again changed it back to a plea of second degree murder. Now she admitted the killing, but insisted she had simply been a pawn in Marchand's plot to kill his wife and said that she had done everything out of love for him.

After months of confusion, Jimerson was acquitted on February 28, 1931. Nancy Bowen, the women who had actually committed the fatal attack, pleaded guilty to reduced charges of first degree manslaughter and on March 13, 1931, was sentenced to a one to ten-year prison sentence. Because she already had been detained in jail for longer than the amount of the minimum sentence, she was allowed to go free.

Winnie Ruth Judd

Sharing an apartment with friends is often difficult, especially if they begin helping themselves to your belongings. However, as Agnes Ann LeRoi and Helwig Samuelson found out, if your roommate should decide that you are stealing their boyfriends then the payback can be horrifying.

When Winnie Ruth Judd, Agnes Ann LeRoi, and Helwig Samuelson—three unmarried girls— decided to share an apartment in Phoenix, Arizona, in 1931, everything went well at first. Like many young women living with friends, they enjoyed each other's company, borrowed clothes, and swapped gossip. Sadly, the easy-going atmosphere wasn't to last. Winnie was somewhat promiscuous and brought a stream of men back to the apartment. Agnes and Helwig objected. The three women had fierce arguments, and Winnie began to believe that her friends were putting obstacles in her way because they wanted her boyfriends for themselves. As her rage and jealousy mounted, she became more and more convinced that Agnes and Helwig were sleeping with the men that rightfully belonged to her.

On October 16, 1931, she snapped, and furiously demanded why the pair kept ruining her relationships. In the circumstances her roommates did the worst thing they possibly could have: they laughed at Winnie. She then shot them both dead.

Working with remarkable presence of mind for a young woman who had just committed a double murder, Winnie immediately put a bullet through her own hand in order to be able to claim self-defense should she be caught. Then she set about disposing of the bodies. Her plan was to dump them into the ocean in her home state of California, and she packed the corpses of her friends into a large trunk for transport, then booked a ticket on a train. When a porter came to collect it he complained it was too heavy and demanded that she instead put "the medical books"— as she described the contents—into smaller cases. Winnie solved the problem by sawing the bodies into pieces.

Incredibly, the cases got as far as California without incident and remained at the station while Winnie fetched her brother to help her with them, telling him brazenly, "There are two bodies in these trunks and the less you know about it, the better off you are." Winnie's plan now began to unravel. A baggage clerk smelled the distinctive odor of rotting flesh coming from the cases, and suspected Winnie and her brother of being meat smugglers. He asked them to open the cases, but Winnie told him she didn't have the keys. Fearing that she was moments from discovery, she grabbed her brother's arm and walked away briskly. As the pair drove away, the clerk made a note of the car registration plate. Then he called the police, still thinking that the worst crime that had been committed was the transport of contraband meat. His mistake was soon corrected in the most horrific manner imaginable. Detectives broke into the cases to find the putrid rotting corpses of two young women.

The hunt was on for a murderer, and Winnie couldn't keep ahead of the law for long. The police traced her brother's car and, meanwhile, the wound in Winnie's hand had become infected. She was forced to attend a hospital and, her cover blown, was arrested.

In court, Winnie maintained her painfully concocted story of self-defense, telling the jury that Helwig had shot her first and that she had then wrestled the gun away from her assailant. The fact that Winnie was now armed hadn't deterred her roommates, and Agnes and Helwig both attacked her again. In fear for her life, Winnie had shot them both.

BELOW: Winnie Ruth Judd (centre), being returned to prison after one of her many escapes.

No one believed her. Winnie Judd was found guilty of the murders of Agnes Ann Le Roi and Helwig Samuelson and sentenced to death. But still she tried to evade justice. While in prison awaiting execution, Winnie's behavior convinced doctors that she was actually insane and not responsible for her crimes. At mental hearing, she put on a fine performance; pretending to hear voices, mumbling incoherently, and pulling at her hair and clothes. The death sentence was commuted to a life of imprisonment in the Arizona state mental institution. Winnie proved sane enough to manage to escape from the secure hospital several times, at one time staying on the run for seven years during which time she worked as a housekeeper. Winnie was finally released on December 22, 1971, 40 years after her deadly fit of jealousy.

Thomas Andrew Keir

The tale of Australian Thomas Andrew Keir is a confusing one, for while awaiting trial for the murder of his second wife, Rosalina Canonizado, police unearthed the remains of his first wife Jean beneath his home in New South Wales. While he was found not guilty of murdering Rosalina, his first wife came back to haunt him and, after various appeals, he would eventually serve time for her killing.

Keir married his first wife Jean in August 1984 when he was 26 and Jean was 18. Four years later, Keir claimed that his wife had run off with another man, leaving their three-year-old son behind. A few weeks after reporting his wife's disappearance, Keir met Rosalina Canonizado while in Sydney attending a family wedding. He divorced Jean on the grounds of desertion and married Rosalina in the Philippines in 1989. Then, on April 13, 1991, Rosalina was found murdered in the same house where Jean had once lived. She had been strangled with a lamp cord and then set on fire. Keir was charged with murder, the prosecution giving a substantial life insurance policy as his motive. But, believing Keir's claims that he was out shopping at the time of the murder, a jury found him not guilty on April 6, 1993. However, while Keir was awaiting trial in prison in 1991, police received information which led to them digging beneath Keir's house where they found fragments of human bone. DNA testing revealed them to belong to Jean Keir.

On September 17, 1999, Thomas Keir was found guilty of Jean Keir's murder in the New South Wales Supreme Court and sentenced to 24 years imprisonment comprising a minimum term of 18 years and an additional term of six years. The court was told Keir killed his 22-year-old wife in a jealous rage after discovering her infidelity. However, the trial judge did not mention Rosalina Canonizado's case during Keir's sentencing. Subsequently, on February 28, 2002, the New South Wales Criminal Court of Appeal revoked Keir's conviction on the grounds that the judge had misdirected the jury regarding the DNA evidence. At this first appeal the judge reduced Keir's sentence by two years to 22 years imprisonment with a non-parole period of 16 years.

A new trial commenced in July 2002 and on October 17 of that year, Keir was again found guilty of Jean's murder. He successfully appealed a second time because of misconduct on the part of members of the jury, but was once again found guilty of Jean's murder at a third trial in December 2004, and the previous sentence was upheld. The court heard that over a period of years Keir had threatened Jean that he would kill her if she left him or "messed around with somebody else." The day after killing his first wife, Keir "apparently coolly and calmly commenced an extensive course of deception designed to conceal the murder." He later dug up her remains and hid them elsewhere, but seven of Jean's bones were left behind and uncovered when police excavated the yard in 1991.

Keir has been decreed to be eligible for parole in 2014 because of time already served. His later conviction for the murder of his first wife would seem to cast doubt on the verdict of not guilty for the murder of Rosalina Canonizado, but perhaps it could be said that Jean had reached out from beyond the grave and exacted the justice owed to both of Thomas Keir's dead wives.

Ralph Klassen

Ralph Klassen's killing of his second wife caused outrage in Canada in the 1990s, not least because he received such a light sentence. The controversy that followed his trial would see a petition presented to the Canadian parliament in which 15,000 people demanded the provocation defense be abolished.

The 13-year marriage of Ralph and Susan Klassen had long been a stormy one. They had already separated several times, and then reconciled, when they agreed to part for yet another trial separation of six months in October, 1995. Klassen left their Whitehorse home and moved to Alberta while his wife began finding an independent life for herself. In fact, she was relieved to be rid of her husband. His temper and jealousy had become increasingly difficult to live with and Susan found herself enjoying her newly peaceful life and freedom. So much so that when her husband began calling her later that month asking that they reconcile immediately rather than wait for the six months to end, she refused.

Suspecting that his wife was now involved with another man, Ralph Klassen returned to Whitehorse on November 1, and arrived at his old home demanding again that Susan take him back. Again, she refused him.

In the early morning hours of November 2, 1995, Ralph Klassen strangled his 36-year-old wife in the bed of their home, applying so much pressure to her neck that he sprained both his thumbs. He then took a pillowcase and tied it around Susan's neck, permanently cutting off the oxygen flow to her brain. There were no signs of a struggle.

When he was sure she was dead, Klassen wrote a brief note for his wife's supposed lover. It said, "I'm sorry I went into a jealous fit of rage. The image of you and my wife together made me insane." He then drove his car into a truck in a suicide attempt, but survived against the odds. When police arrived on the scene he confessed to killing his wife.

Klassen was charged with second degree murder, but used the Canadian provocation defense to have it dropped to manslaughter. The jury found him guilty on January 17, 1997. For the killing of his wife Ralph Klassen received a sentence of just five years imprisonment. The term was greeted with shock by the public. However, it was also established that he would be eligible for an early release in May, 2000, when only two-thirds of the light sentence had been served.

There was an immediate outcry. A week later more than 300 people marched through Whitehorse to protest and, also spurred on by the sentence, Klassen's first wife also came forward to tell how Klassen had repeatedly assaulted her during their marriage, on one occasion choking her. In response to the outrage on May 27, the Federal Justice Crown appealed against the lenient sentence arguing that it was "inadequate, given the aggravating factors of spousal violence and breach of trust." A month later three judges dismissed the appeal, saying that the five-year sentence was in line with those imposed in similar cases.

While the controversy raged on, and eventually culminated in an appeal to parliament that the law be revised so that others couldn't use the same defense in the future, Ralph Klassen's sentence remained unchanged. As suggested at his trial he was released from the William Head Institution, a medium-security federal penitentiary on Vancouver Island, in 2000.

Ada Le Bouef & Dr. Thomas Dreher

James Le Bouef was allowed to live only so long as he turned a blind eye to his wife's passionate liaison with his best friend. When he began to raise objections that threatened to end the affair his fate was sealed.

In the 1920s, Morgan City in Louisiana's was a simply community of simply country folk. Set in the bayou country of swamps and creeks fed by the waters of the mighty Mississippi River, many Morgan City people lived by trading as frog catchers, trappers, moonshiner's, and alligator hunters. But James and Ada Le Boeuf were a cut above most folk in the area. In a time when electricity was moving from a luxury to a necessity for

BELOW: Lake Palourde, the beauty spot in southern Louisiana where Ada Le Bouef, Thomas Dreher and Jim Beadle dumped the body of Ada's husband.

every home, he was superintendent of the Morgan City Light and Power Company and a man of some standing in the small town.

The Le Bouefs had been long married, with five children, when Ada began suffering from terrible headaches that confined her to bed. Her worried husband immediately called his good friend Dr. Thomas Dreher to ease her pain. At first Le Bouef thought that Dreher was simply attending Ada so frequently out of concern for his wife, but as Ada's headaches began to strike more regularly with Dreher in attendance each time, it became obvious that it wasn't a dose of medicine the doctor was giving her. Nevertheless, Le Bouef didn't have the courage to face the scandal that would follow a confrontation of that kind in such a small town. He discreetly allowed them to continue with their liaison in the hope that it would fizzle out and things could get back to normal.

However, the affair couldn't escape the attention of others for long in such a small community, and the neighborhood was soon abuzz with rumors of adultery taking place at the Le Bouef house and anywhere else Ada and the Dreher could find to meet. An anonymous letter was sent to Dreher's wife, telling her, "Two nights ago there was a lady and a man in that empty shack in the bayou. One of them was Ada Le Boeuf and the other was your husband!" Someone else spread a story that Dreher and Ada had been spotted swimming naked together in the bayou.

James Le Boeuf had been prepared to keep quiet in order to keep his humiliation from becoming public knowledge, but now the secret was out he demanded that the affair stop straight away. But he underestimated the strength of the lovers' passion, and the steps they were prepared to take to preserve it" Le Boeuf's body was pulled out of the bayou in July 1927. He had been shot twice in the head.

The identity of his murderers was obvious, and the police swiftly arrested Ada and her lover. Soon after, they also brought a trapper of dubious reputation named Jim Beadle into custody. He was known to have held a grudge against James Le Boeuf.

All three were tried together at Franklin, Louisiana. Dreher's story was that Ada sent him a note asking him to get rid of her husband. It said that she would be rowing on the local lake with him on July 1, and that would be the time to strike. Dreher called on Beadle and they rowed out together. Dreher claimed it was Beadle who fired the two shots, but the trapper denied it, telling the court that the doctor shot James Le Bouef, after which he had "slit open Le Boeuf's stomach" so that the corpse would sink to the bottom and be hidden forever.

All three were found guilty of murder and conspiracy to commit murder. Dr. Thomas Dreher and Ada La Bouef were given death sentences and were hanged side by side on February 1, 1929. Jim Beadle was jailed for life for his part in the killing.

Thomas Ley

For some, a crime of passion is committed in a burst of terrible anger or jealousy, while for others the jealousy grows in their minds until it drives them literally insane. It was unfortunate for John McMain Mudie that he crossed the path of a man who was completely possessed by his own fevered suspicions.

The body of John Mudie was found in a chalk pit in Surrey, England, on November 30, 1946. He had been beaten and hanged with a dirty rag stuffed in his mouth, then trussed and dumped. He had been a decent man in life; popular and jovial, he had served his country well during World War II and in peacetime had become a barman. His only crime was to take lodgings in a London house that was also shared by Maggie Brook, the long-term mistress of Thomas John Ley, a former Minister of Justice in New Zealand.

The police hunted down the killer quickly and efficiently. The identity card in Mudie's pocket led them straight to his lodgings, and their questions soon revealed a likely suspect, for Ley's terrifying jealousy was well known. And when one of the men who had helped him murder his victim turned Queen's Evidence, the whole story unraveled.

Despite the fact that Maggie Brook was a respectable woman, her lover was obsessed with his suspicions over her conduct. At some point or another he had accused her of sleeping with virtually every man she knew, including those who lodged at the same house. For some inexplicable reason though, he had come to focus his jealousy on Maudie, perhaps simply because Maudie's simple, likeable character was so different from his own dark nature.

Twisted by his suspicions, Ley hatched a plot to remove his rival and recruited carpenter Lawrence Smith and chauffeur John Buckingham to help. A woman friend, Lilian Bruce, was paid to play the role of

OVERLEAF: A 1947 photograph of murderer Thomas John Ley, a former Minister of Justice in New Zealand.

BELOW: The chalkpit at Woldingham in Surrey where the body of barman John Mudie was discovered in 1946.

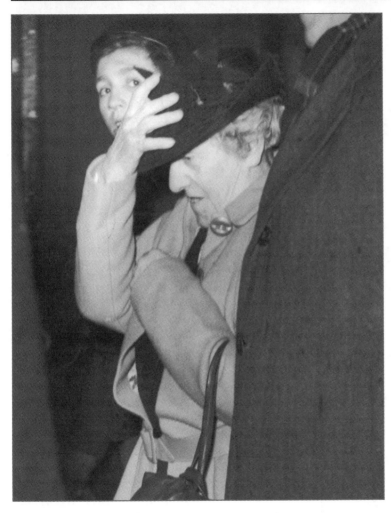

LEFT: Mrs Emily Ley, the wife Thomas John Ley, arriving at Waterloo Station from Australia, to attend her husband's trial.

OVERLEAF: John Buckingham being helped into his car by his son (left) after giving evidence at the Old Bailey, London, in the trial of Thomas John Ley

When Buckingham heard about the discovery of John Mudie's body he went straight to the police. He had stayed outside with the car and had no knowledge that he had been part of a murder. All charges against him were dropped, and he later testified against Ley and Smith. Police also learned that the two men had been paid in one pound notes, the exact amount and denomination that had been withdrawn from Ley's bank that very day.

The four-day trial started on March 19, 1947, with both Ley and Smith pleading not guilty. Nevertheless, the case against them was unanswerable, and so dreadful was the crime against an innocent man that the death sentence was passed. Before he was hanged though, Ley was declared insane and given a reprieve. That presented a legal dilemma; if the man who organized such a brutal murder was not going to be executed, how could the man who had been paid to help face the death sentence? Smith was reprieved too and sentenced to life imprisonment. Within four months of his arrival at the top security mental institute of Broadmoor in Berkshire, Ley died of a brain haemorrhage.

a wealthy woman who seemed to be attracted to Mudie and so lure him back to her home in a chauffer-driven car—with Buckingham at the wheel. The house they arrived at, however, was not hers, but Ley's. Once inside, Mudie was attacked by Ley and Smith, severely beaten, and hanged with a cord. Ley then handed Smith and Buckingham £200 cash each for their efforts—and for their silence.

Ann Marie Linscott

Fortunately for the wife of her lover, Ann Marie Linscott's plot to assassinate her was discovered before it could do any harm. Nevertheless, it is an interesting case and one that shows how crimes of passion might adapt to the digital age.

The age of the internet has resulted in many curious affairs. Many people who would never otherwise have met have developed intense passions for each other in cyberspace and in numerous cases a liaison conducted in virtual reality has had a disastrous effect on real-life relationships. One such affair began in 2004 when Ann Marie Linscott met a man whose identity has never been revealed in an internet chat room. Ann Marie was 49, a wife, and mother to two teenage children, but thoughts of her family were far from her mind as the online lovers tapped out messages of lust on their keyboards.

Eventually, they managed to contrive a meeting. In 2005, the man involved was sent to a conference in Reno, Nevada. Ann Marie joined him there and at last their passion became physical. The brief sexual encounter only served to deepen their intimacy, and the pair continued the relationship by phone and email, the enforced separation serving only to fan the flames of passion, for Ann Marie especially. Although she and her lover managed to meet again, it was not enough for Ann Marie and she hatched a plot to make the man she adored single. It proved to be as stupid as it was potentially deadly.

In November 2007, three California residents were separately searching the website craigslist.com for job opportunities when they came across an advert that looked interesting. The job was described only as a "freelance" position and each of them asked for more information. They began exchanging emails with Ann Marie Linscott, who used an alias, and it soon became apparent that the freelance position was a crude code for a contract killer.

Linscott asked each of the three job applicants to "eradicate" a woman living in Butte County, California, and provided a description of the victim, her age, and the address where she worked. On two occasions she offered payment of $5,000 upon completion of the task. Realizing that she was deadly serious, all three of the jobseekers reported the mystery employer to the police.

Californian detectives quickly established the identity of the intended victim and discovered that she was married. Under questioning, the details of her husband's infidelity were revealed, and the trail finally led them to Ann Marie. Background checks on her revealed a list of irregularities: She had once taken out a restraining order on one of her colleagues, and he had responded in kind, claiming that she had made unwanted advances. She had also given false information on her resume, saying that she had worked as a massage therapist at a hospital that had never heard of her.

Linscott was arrested at her home in January 2008 and charged with perpetrating a murder-for-hire scheme. On February 4, 2009, she was found guilty and sentenced to 12 years and seven months in prison. The judge hearing the case condemned Linscott for showing no remorse and said the heavy sentence was to protect the public from people like her, and to deter anyone else who might be considering using the internet to recruit a killer. Strangely, her husband, John, supported her throughout.

Denise Labbe & Jacques Algarron

This crime of passion is unusual, and more sickening than most. It was not committed out of revenge or in the heat of the moment, but against a complete innocent whose mother had the misfortune to come under the spell of a philosophy student whose beliefs were nothing short of insane. He abused her love for him by asking her to prove it in the most vile way imaginable.

Denise Labbe's life had often been a struggle, but she had worked hard to better herself. She was the daughter of a poor postman and after being orphaned at 13 had educated herself to the point where she was able to land a job as a secretary. She also allowed herself a little fun along the way, usually with the male students of her home town of Rennes, France, and by the time she reached 25, she had a toddler daughter called Catherine. Nevertheless, she was coping well with life's demands until she met a charismatic graduate of philosophy named Jacques Algarron. He was three years her junior and seduced her with the line he always used on women: "I offer you fervor." She was immediately bewitched by the complex and well-read young man and began a passionate affair with him.

Algarron was a great admirer philosophy that suggested the existence of "super humans" and told his new girlfriend that he believed they were a super couple. Unfortunately, his demented ideas quickly grew into an obsession. He needed Denise to prove that she was superior to other women and worthy of his love. The scheme Algarron hit upon should have told Denise that he was an extremely dangerous individual, but she was head over heels in love and couldn't bear the idea

ABOVE: Jacques Algarron, being escorted in a police car on the second day of his trial in Blois, France.

that she might lose him. Algarron read Denise a story in which a mother kills her child by another man to please her lover and told her how beautiful it was. She had to suffer, too, he said. The deluded Denise agreed, convinced by what she saw as Algarron's high intellect and advanced philosophy.

Her first attempt to kill Catherine wasn't successful. Appalled by the enormity of what she was about to do and disturbed by the appearance of a neighbor, Denise found that she could not drop her daughter from a window as planned. Her second went little better. Denise threw Catherine into a canal, only to be overwhelmed by her maternal instinct to protect her child. She summoned help, and the little girl was pulled out of the water by a passerby.

By now Algarron was becoming impatient and threatened to leave her if she did not carry out his orders. So, on November 8, 1954, she drowned Catherine in a washtub then telegraphed Algarron to tell him that she had done as asked. He later told a friend, "It takes courage to kill your own daughter."

The child's disappearance soon aroused suspicions among Denise's neighbors, and police were called in to question her. She confessed to the horrific crime, but told them that Algarron was to blame.

The thunder and lightning that accompanied the opening of the trial of Denise Labbe and Jacques Algarron was seen as a sign of their demonic possession. Both were found guilty of murder with Denise sentenced to life imprisonment and Algarron to 20 years. Algarron, however, had a final statement to the court and pompously stood to deliver it. "Certain monsters," he told the stunned people in the room, "are sacred because often the same qualities are found in a monster and in a saint." Like the horrendous crime he had incited Denise to commit, it was beyond anyone's comprehension.

Adolph Luetgert

The trial of Adolph Luetgert for the murder of his wife Louise in 1897 became one of the first in the United States to be carried out under the full glare of the media and with the nation eagerly awaiting every grisly new revelation. It was hardly surprising as the case had all the elements of a penny dreadful story: infidelity, violence, murder, and a particularly grisly method for deposing of the body.

The trial of Adolph Luetgert for the murder of his wife Louise in 1897 became one of the first in the United States to be carried out under the full glare of the media and with the nation eagerly awaiting every grisly new revelation. It was hardly surprising as the case had all the elements of a penny dreadful story: infidelity, violence, murder, and a particularly grisly method for deposing of the body.

Like many of the marriages within these pages, Adolph and Louise Luetgerts' was not a happy one. He was the owner of a sausage factory and she was his second wife, but the fact that he was married did not stop him conducting numerous affairs and during their frequent arguments, during which Louise would implore her husband to stop sleeping with other women, Luetgert often became violent. In fact, neighbors once reported seeing Luetgert trying to strangle his wife, stopping only when he realized he was being watched.

On May 1, 1897, when her brother came looking for her, Luetgert admitted that Louise had disappeared. He claimed that she had left him and that he didn't know where she had gone, but her brother was suspicious. He informed the police who took Luetgert in for questioning, asking him why he had not reported her missing when the year before he had come to them for help when his dog disappeared. Luetgert maintained that he had hired a private detective to find his wife, fearing a scandal if his marital problems became public.

No one believed him and after a witness came forward to say they had seen Luetgert leading his wife into a back alley by his factory on April 24, a search for her body began. At first a nearby river was trawled, but when that proved fruitless the police turned their attentions to the factory itself and soon uncovered some gruesome evidence: fragments of human bone and a wedding ring with the initials "LL" in one of the vats. They also found a night watchman, who had unwittingly helped with the boiling up of Louise Luetgert and had been curious about the strange slime he had been asked to dispose of. He later testified that Luetgert had told him, "Don't say a word and I'll see you have a good job as long as you live."

The press went wild. Newspapers fought one another for scoops, people across the country claimed to have seen the missing woman alive, and each new clue led to fresh rounds of speculation about the crime. Meanwhile, sausage sales plummeted nationwide as rumors circulated that Luetgert had destroyed his wife's body in one of his factory's meat grinders. In fact, the rest of her body was never found and it is impossible to say what went on in the factory.

At Luetgert's trial, witnesses came forward to speak of his violent tendencies and letters from his various mistresses were read out. They suggested that Luetgert had promised to marry other women and share his fortune, though he was actually on the verge of bankruptcy. Through it all, Luetgert maintained his innocence, telling the jury that one day Louise would return to him. Despite his protestations, the evidence against him was overwhelming. Adolph Luetgert was found guilty of the murder of his wife and sentenced to life. He died in the Joliet State Penitentiary in 1899.

BELOW: Joliet State Penitentiary, in Illinois, where Adolph Luetgert served his life sentence for the murder of his wife.

Harmohinder Kaur Sanghera

When Sair Ali got married to his 17-year-old cousin, he didn't bother to trouble his existing lover with the news. But when she finally found out that he had been cheating on her with a new wife, Harmohinder's jealousy and anger drove her to a terrible revenge.

When Sair Ali got married to his 17-year-old cousin, he didn't bother to trouble his existing lover with the news. But when she finally found out that he had been cheating on her with a new wife, Harmohinder's jealousy and anger drove her to a terrible revenge.

Harmohinder Kaur Sanghera and Sair Ali met in 2005 when she was 23, and he 25. Instantly attracted to one another they began a passionate affair, kept secret to avoid scandal among their respective communities— Harmohinder was a Sikh, Ali came from a strict Muslim family. However, completely unbeknown to Harmohinder, her lover was already betrothed to his cousin Sana, and when they were married in Pakistan Ali still did not confess.

Nevertheless, Harmohinder's suspicions were aroused when Ali's passion for seemed to cool. They no longer met so often and when they did, he seemed distant. The reason, she was later to discover, was not only did Ali have a wife but she was already four month's pregnant.

Furious that the man she loved could keep such an enormous secret from her, Harmohinder decided that if her own happiness was to be destroyed, then Ali's would be too. She told a friend that the following day she intended to confront Sana with the truth about her husband's adulterous affair and then end the relationship with him for good. But over the next 24 hours she appears to have changed her plan.

Harmohinder drove to the couple's home in Bury, Lancashire, armed with a knife and stabbed Sana to death in a frenzied attack as she lay in her bedroom. Examiners would later find 43 knife wounds on the body, among which was a deep abdomen wound that had obviously been intended to destroy the 11-week foetus of Sana's baby boy. Harmohinder then calmly climbed through a kitchen window, secured the house, and drove back to her home in Birmingham.

Like many first-time murderers, Harmohinder was quickly discovered. Her footprints were found at the scene, and proof that she had travelled to Birmingham that day was easily gathered from CCTV cameras that lined the roads she had used. She was found guilty of murder in November 2007 and sentenced to life, to serve a minimum of 14 years.

Nevertheless, Harmohinder's revenge had found its target. The cheating Sair Ali lost both his wife and child. Although no one could ever deserve the punishment that Harmohinder meted out, Ali must have known that if his own behavior had been different the crime might well have been averted. As he later said, "No one can sleep. We all have nightmares. We cannot stay in the house now. No one can go into Sana's bedroom; the door is always closed. Her clothes still hang in her wardrobe. We can't face it yet and don't feel we ever can."

Larissa Schuster

Since dubbed the "Mad Chem Chick" by the press at the time of her arrest Larissa Schuster seemed the least likely of murderers. Stout, bottle blonde, and 42 years old, she was a successful businesswoman and devoted mother. The method she chose to despatch her husband was so sickening that it shocked the United States. Her story is a complex one but perfectly illustrates what can happen when love turns to ashes.

Larissa Schuster's background gave no hints that one day she would become a murderer. She was born on a farm in Missouri and raised by parents who taught her strong Christian values. She was, as a court was to hear many years later, a "happy and normal child" with a love of animals and people.

At college, Schuster appears to have been a popular A-grade student and a star baseball player. After learning to drive she became a volunteer hospital worker. If there was a flaw in her character it was that she had expectations of others that sometimes could not be fulfilled, expectations that saw her first serious relationship end disastrously.

BELOW: Larissa Schuster listening to evidence being given at a hearing in a Los Angeles County courthouse during her trial for the murder of her husband.

Despite the painful break-up with her first boyfriend, Larissa pulled herself together and while still at college fell in love again, this time with a young man called Tim Schuster, who she met and married shortly before graduating with honors. The couple set out on a married life that was full of promise. He was a registered nurse, she a bright graduate quickly taken on to perform research for the pesticide industry by ABC Laboratories in Columbia, Missouri. In 1985, they were blessed with a daughter, Kristin, and four years later Larissa was offered the job of laboratory manager for the Pan Am airline in California. The family moved to Fresno, California, and in 1990 Larissa gave birth to their son, Tyler.

To the outside world Tim and Larissa's family life looked like the fulfilment of the American dream; they were comfortably off and regular churchgoers with a wide circle of friends. If Larissa had suffered from a lack of self-confidence in her younger years, success at work had given her a new poise. But behind closed doors, as is so often the case, the relationship was not all it seemed. Over the years, Tim Schuster had gradually begun treating his wife with more and more contempt. He belittled her efforts at her job and constantly reminded her of her poor, rural upbringing. The couple bickered and argued often, and though beneath it all Larissa still loved her husband, their house had a constant atmosphere of tension and mistrust. In court, she would later describe her home life thus: "Everything seemed fine on the surface; trying to do good and admirable things, but the problem was the interior of the marriage. It was surviving but still had problems."

In fact, the marriage was breaking down fast. The Schusters' sex life had dwindled and, unhappy at home, Larissa threw herself into work. Often tired and irritable as well as suffering

from the constant strain of a difficult marriage, she tried to maintain some kind of order in the house by being a strict disciplinarian with the children. In turn, they developed behavior problems, something Larissa had to deal with on her own. Kristin was sent off to live with her grandparents in Missouri in a bid to give her a more settled home life.

Amazingly, in this pressured environment the Schuster's marriage struggled on for another 12 years, during which time Larissa invested much of her emotional energies into work. Eventually, she opened her own business, Central California Research Laboratories, and came to be respected as one of the top chemists in the country. Nevertheless, the unhealthy marriage had become increasingly poisonous. By now the Schusters could not even look at each other, and Larissa confided in a friend that she genuinely hated her husband. Something had to give, and Larissa finally asked Tim for a divorce.

To her surprise, he refused to even acknowledge the request, let alone move out of the family home, and the marriage limped on until Larissa noticed that her husband had started keeping a journal. Her curiosity was aroused and she sneaked a look one night to find that Tim had been writing damning entries about her emotional state and inability to care for the children or her business. He had also noted actions that could be

LEFT: A handcuffed James Fagone being led from court after a guilty verdict was read in his trial.

interpreted as signs of mental problems. Larissa jumped to the obvious conclusion—her business was doing well and Tim was preparing to wage a bitter divorce battle to take the children and as much money as possible.

After more angry scenes, Tim finally left the family home in July 2002. He was awarded custody of their son and took away every stick of furniture and every possession while Larissa was away visiting her parents and Kristin. By now, her mental state had begun to unravel. All the love she had once felt turned to a bitter loathing. She began making vicious, angry calls to her husband, up to eight times a day, calling him names, mocking his sexual performance, and telling him that he was a terrible father to their children.

The divorce dragged on. A year later the couple were still fighting over their share in Larissa's business, with Tim wanting a million dollars as a settlement. The emotional turmoil was also taking a toll on their children. In an attempt to find a little peace for them and herself, she took Tyler to visit his sister and grandparents in Missouri. Tim Schuster retaliated by calling the police and accusing his wife of kidnapping their son.

In the middle of all this confusion Larissa had found a friend and confidante. James Fagone was a young laboratory assistant. Lazy, lacking in ambition, and with a variety of personal problems of his own, it is probably a sign of her state of mind that Larissa didn't recognize immediately that he was a deeply disturbed individual. Nevertheless, he proved useful and was often at her house clearing the yard, walking the family dog, and generally helping out. Larissa found that she could

talk to the young man and often, of course, their conversations revolved around her problems with the divorce and her hatred of her husband. Fagone assured her of his own disgust at Tim Schuster and promised to help whatever the circumstances.

What finally caused Larissa to snap was a fairly trivial incident by the standards of her acrimonious marriage and divorce. She wanted to take Tyler to Disneyland and then on a visit to Missouri. Tim scuppered it. It proved to be the final straw. Now, Larissa just wanted her husband dead.

In the early hours of July 10, 2003, Fagone and Larissa went to Tim's home and fired a stun gun at him as he opened the door. They then dragged him through the house, held a chloroform-soaked rag to his mouth, and tied him up before loading him into a truck and driving him to Larissa's house. What happened next outraged the court and the American public. While still alive, Tim Schuster was shoved head-first into a 55-gallon plastic barrel, then Larissa and her accomplice poured hydrochloric acid over him and sealed the barrel.

Two days later Fagone and Larissa drove the barrel to her Fresno business premises. She poured in more acid, but had trouble resealing the lid so she used a handsaw to cut off her husband's feet. However, Larissa knew that the incriminating barrel couldn't remain somewhere so obvious. She organized a storage unit and called her friend to ask him to remove it, but by that time even the deranged Fagone had had enough by now and fled the area.

Police were alerted to Tim Schuster's disappearance when the normally obsessively punctual man failed to turn up for appointments. A search of his home quickly established that something was amiss. There was no sign of Tim, but his wallet and mobile phone remained in the house. Further enquiries led to interviews with staff at Larissa's laboratory. Investigators heard of the hatred between the couple, their multi-million dollar divorce, the custody battle, and how Larissa had often been heard to say that she wished her husband was dead. Larissa immediately became the prime suspect.

While it was already obvious to the police that they had found their killer, investigations continued. At the laboratory, staff told of how Larissa had joked that her husband's body might fit into the 55-gallon barrel. And when they went to show it to officers were surprised to find it had vanished. Another employee told them that Larissa had asked him to rent a truck and a storage unit in his name so that she might hide some property from her husband until the divorce was final. When she had returned the truck, the employee noticed blood on one of Larissa's shoes.

Over the next couple of days, police searched Larissa Schuster's home, her offices and laboratory, and the self-storage unit. They unearthed several items including blond wigs and bloody tennis shoes from Schuster's home; and Fagone's time sheets, chemical order invoices, saws, and a mop and bucket from the business. And when they opened the self-storage unit they found what remained of Tim Schuster. Partially dismembered and decomposing, the corpse was later described as "intact from only the belt buckle down."

Police arrested Fagone on July 15, 2003, and Schuster the next day. Three days later, detectives searched Fagone's home and seized receipts for a stun gun and a 14-inch cable tie, bank statements, folding buck knife, and computer equipment.

Under questioning, it immediately became apparent that Larissa's mental state was completely breaking down. One moment she expressed sickness at the atrocity she had committed on the man she once loved, the next she was desperate not to let Tyler down by missing the promised trip to Disneyland.

Fagone and Schuster first appeared in court on September 29, 2003. Then followed another hearing at Fresno County Court where the couple pleaded innocent to charges of murder with special circumstances—torture, murder during a kidnapping, lying in wait to commit murder, and murder for financial gain. The Fresno County District Attorney's Office later added a fifth special circumstance—that the pair murdered Timothy Schuster during a burglary. If convicted of the murder and any of the special circumstances, the law could impose the death penalty.

While the killers awaited trial in jail, the police and lawyers took almost three years to carefully compile their evidence and prepare for court. The case of James Fagone, by now aged 25, finally came before a judge on November 25, 2006, at Fresno County Court. The prosecution had prepared well and a judgement was reached quickly. His guilty verdict was read out on December 11. Fagone was given life imprisonment with no chance of parole on February 20, 2007. On hearing the sentence he muttered, "I humbly ask the court for your forgiveness."

The trial of Larissa Schuster began at Los Angeles County Court on October 15, 2007. Roger Nuttall, her defense lawyer, attempted to paint Larissa as a victim of circumstances, a woman who had tried her best to maintain order amid terrible emotional stress, and eventually failed. He described her as "a very committed mother, talented individual, and a very lovely human being." The prosecution, however, argued that Schuster was a domineering woman who repeatedly made threats against her husband and that Fagone had only become her accomplice because she intimidated him. Nuttall responded by repeatedly questioning the validity of Fagone's evidence.

Schuster's case lasted longer than that of her accomplice. Nevertheless, she was finally found guilty in December 2007 and, like Fagone, was sentenced to life without parole on May 16, 2008. Judge Wayne Ellison told her that her attorneys were to be thanked for saving her life. He commented, "This is the kind of case in which the jury may have imposed the death penalty, and this court might have upheld the imposition of that penalty. In the light of everything Mr Nuttall has said, it is true to say, he saved your life."

Carolyn Warmus

A wealthy, if unhappy, family life gave Carolyn Warmus a sense of entitlement from an early age. Later, it would begin to show in bizarre behavior if one of her many affairs didn't go exactly as she expected; behavior that would come to a tragic climax when her latest married lover dumped her.

Carolyn Warmus was born in January 1964 and grew up in Birmingham, Michigan, a rich suburb of Detroit. Her parents divorced when she was just eight years old and by the time she began attending the University of Michigan it was obvious to those who came close to her that she had psychological problems. She seemed desperate for physical and emotional contact, but one by one all of her relationships broke down because of her possessiveness. Finally, one former boyfriend, Paul Laven, was forced to take out a restraining order to keep Carolyn away from him. The obsessive behavior continued when Carolyn moved to New York, where she hired a private detective to follow a married bartender who had also had the nerve to end their relationship.

Despite her emotional problems, Carolyn eventually earned a master's degree in elementary education from Columbia University and landed a job in September 1987, at the Greenville Elementary in Scarsdale, New

OVERLEAF: The two-story Scarsdale apartment complex where murderer Carolyn Warmus allegedly shot her lover's wife before meeting him for sex in a parking lot.

BELOW: High school yearbook picture of future murderer Carolyn Warmus (center) who would kill her lover's wife eight years later.